PATH OF FREEDOM

BUILDING MINDFULNESS-BASED EMOTIONAL INTELLIGENCE

BY K. VITA PIRES-CRISP

ILLUSTRATIONS BY ART REID + SAMO SKERBEC

PRISON DHARMA PRESS

PATH OF FREEDOM

BUILDING MINDFULNESS-BASED EMOTIONAL
INTELLIGENCE BY KATE PIRES-CRISP

First edition November 2006
Second edition July 2012
Third edition November 2017
Fourth edition November 2018
Fifth edition: April 2020

Cover and Book Design by K.Vita Pires-Crisp

Prison Dharma Press
Prison Mindfulness Institute
www.PrisonMindfulness.org
PO Box 206
South Deerfield, MA 01373

Printed in the United States of America
ISBN: 09718143-2-5

CONTENTS

"We're all just walking each other home."
Ram Dass, Author

I. TRAINING THE MIND
THE POWER OF MINDFULNESS

THE PATH OF TROUBLE

The Path of Trouble can seem like fun when we first get on it. It may even look like it's our only choice in life.

And then:
- The thrill dies and the mess begins.
- Anxiety, crazy looping thoughts, anger, fear, conflict, confusion and addictions happen.
- You're stuck!

PATH OF FREEDOM

On the Path of Freedom one will find tools to:

- Make friends with our mind and emotions,
- Get unstuck from being lost in negativity and confusion,
- Move out of the shadows of drama and trauma.

THE POWER OF MINDFULNESS

Mindfulness Meditation is our best ally on the Path of Freedom.

LEARNING TO MEDITATE WILL HELP YOU:

- Deal with looping thoughts & upset feelings,
- Change reactions that make trouble,
- Reduce stress & calm your mind,
- Become clear & focused,
- Make healthier choices,
- Decrease drama in relationships.

WHAT IS MINDFULNESS?

Mindfulness is the skill of being awake, alert and focused in the present moment. Have you ever noticed that you are somewhere doing something and you don't even remember how you got there? Sometimes it may even seem like you are sleepwalking through your own life. With mindfulness, you are back on the planet and on target. Right now you are reading this sentence. Does your mind wander as you read? Do you leap ahead to look at the picture?

ZING! HERE YOU ARE !

Just sitting still, meditating (eyes shut or open), will train you to

WAKE UP!

THINKING . . . THINKING . . . THINKING . .

Almost every moment of the day, our minds are thinking. Thoughts come and go, racing around in our heads endlessly. Most of us build our lives around the stories we create in our heads. Even one small, anxious thought can grab us and turn into a huge, disturbing story (in our minds). We believe our thoughts are real, true and solid, even though, on some level, they are just things we are telling ourselves in our own heads.

Meditation is not about getting rid of thoughts; thoughts are useful. It's the looping, anxious thoughts we allow to become solid and stuck that can create problems, leading to harmful speech and unskillful actions. In meditation, the practice of labeling thoughts as "Thinking" will help us put those thoughts into a bigger space so that we can relax and not get so wrapped up in them.

Thoughts are like birds in the sky, we don't necessarily need to capture and cage them in the brain and turn them into projects, by going around trying to convince ourselves (or others) that our thoughts are the "truth?" Thoughts might be true, they also might be just thoughts changing into other different thoughts. In meditation, practice labeling thoughts "Thinking," will help you to see thoughts as changeable, and see that sometimes we can even just let them fly by, dissolving into space.

TRAINING THE MIND

The mind is a tricky thing. It is often like a monkey, swinging from branch to branch, grasping from thoughts to worries. Practicing mindfulness meditation trains the mind to settle and be calm.

PRACTICE, PRACTICE, PRACTICE . . .

Training the mind takes time, discipline, and practice. One can think of training the mind the same way you train muscles. Both take time and practice, require repetitions and can be hard. And, just like weight training, once the muscles are built, we need to maintain them by practicing daily.

10

THE GRIP OF EMOTIONS

If you grip something, the muscles in your hand and arm tense. If you continue to grip, your entire body tenses. Relax the hand and the tension leaves. The mind grabs at thoughts and worries. The longer we grip onto these thoughts and stories, the more tense and agitated our mind becomes. Meditation trains the mind, over and over, to relax the grip on thoughts and emotions.

TAKING CHARGE

Mindfulness is a tool that helps us when we are lost, distracted, or 'taken over' by thoughts and emotions. Instead of being imprisoned by our thoughts, feelings, or impulses, mindfulness will allow us to take charge of our own mind, reactions and emotions rather than having them take charge of us.

IT IMPROVES OUR GAME

The Los Angeles Lakers, the Chicago Bulls, and the New York Knicks all use meditation to improve performance. Coaches say that meditation helps players be more centered, focused, and aware—qualities that result in a more successful game.

"I do mindfulness practice in the morning.
It's the first thing I do when I get up.
It's the best way to kick off the day to get me in balance."
Kobe Bryant, L.A. Lakers, R.I.P.

RELAXING VS. REACTING

Have you ever been told that you are "too impulsive" or "out of control"? Do you react so fast that you don't have time to think about what might actually happen when you do something?

Meditation helps us slow down and have space to think about our choices before jumping into action. It lets us hit the pause button so we can act from a strong and clear place.

WHAT MEDITATION IS:

- A way to find peace,
- A tool to help us be less reactive,
- A way to deal with stress and tension,
- Something that can help--anywhere, anytime, in any situation.

WHAT MEDITATION IS NOT:

- A quick fix,
- A way to get rid of thoughts,
- A way to avoid emotions.

STRESS + RELAXATION

In meditation, you use the breath to relax. Breath can affect you powerfully. Next time you are tense or stressed, see if your breath is fast and shallow and/or if your muscles are tight. Then try breathing deeply and slowly into your belly. Try it for a few minutes. See if that helps you be more relaxed and calm. Experiment with it.

EXERCISE:

Take a moment right now, stop, shut your eyes, and take four, slow, deep breaths . . .

What happened?
Did you notice any change?
How do you feel?

HOW TO PRACTICE MEDITATION:

SIX POINTS OF GOOD POSTURE

1. SEAT:
Sit comfortably on the floor or on a chair. Your posture should be alert and awake (not slumping). If cross-legged, your knees shouldn't be higher than your hips (use a blanket or pillow if needed).

2. LEGS:
If on the floor, cross your legs at the ankles. If in a chair, plant your feet firmly on the floor, hip-width apart. If your legs cramp or fall asleep, it is okay to stretch them out or briefly bring your knees up.

3. ARMS:
Relax your shoulders. Let your arms hang loosely. Rest your hands comfortably on your thighs, palms down.

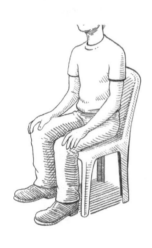

4. STRONG BACK/SOFT FRONT:
Your torso is upright and dignified, as if you are a king or queen on a throne.
Spine=strong and straight.
Chest=soft and open.

5. EYES:
Your eyes can be open or shut. If open, gaze softly down about three to four feet in front of you.

6. MOUTH:
Relax your face and jaw. Your

mouth should be slightly open. Place the tongue on the roof of the mouth.

7. FOCUS ON BREATH:
Take a few deep breaths, exhaling fully. Let your breath settle into its natural rhythm. Keep your focus on the breath. If you get distracted, gently bring your attention back to the breath.

The breath is the one thing that is always with you. Use this tool anytime to calm down and make better choices. The more you practice, the more it will show up for you when you need it.

8. LABEL THOUGHTS "THINKING":
As you meditate, your mind may wander, and thoughts, emotions, or distractions may appear. The point of meditation is not to get rid of thoughts, push them away, or make a big deal out of them. When you notice you are thinking, simply say to yourself (silently) "Thinking."

Let the thoughts go, and gently come back to your breath. Don't beat yourself up for thinking. Thoughts are not 'good' or 'bad'. Whether you are thinking about hitting someone or thinking about lunch, simply label it 'Thinking' and return to your breath. This is mind training that will allow you to realize that you don't need to act on, or be controlled by every thought that pops up in your mind. Thoughts are not necessarily solid truth, they are sometimes simply just thoughts.

YOUR BREATH IS YOUR ALLY

Early one morning, I was co-teaching a meditation class at the local county jail. The class was located in a tiny room with a giant picture window facing a busy, noisy hallway.   Soon after we started the class, the guards lined up some prisoners just outside the window. The guys in the line peeped in the windows, making faces and laughing at the folks in our class.

On top of that distraction, the already small room was divided into two rooms with a moveable divider. Our group was on one side, and the "Anger Management" class was on the other. The Anger Management folks were definitely working through some anger issues quite loudly that morning.   Despite all of the noise and distractions from the 'outside' world, most of the eight guys in our class sat quietly, meditating and respectfully asking us questions about meditation.

One guy in the class, however, was really rowdy. He didn't appear to have the slightest interest in meditation. He was making all sorts of wisecrack comments, interrupting everyone, and at one point, started rolling around on the floor (really!), laughing his head off for no apparent reason. He seemed   to be doing just about anything other than meditating or listening to our instructions on how to meditate. He didn't attempt to settle down during the entire class.

To wrap up the class, my co-teacher made this statement in a rather serious and dramatically loud tone of voice: "Listen up, guys! You may never come to this class again and we may never see any of you again. You may never go to a meditation group again or even ever meditate again, but remember just this one thing:
Your Breath is your Ally.

The next week I was quite surprised to see that 'Roll on the Floor Laughing during Meditation guy' showed up to class. He seemed very excited and wanted to tell us all something.

"Guess what?" he said. "Last week, I was up on the third floor tier and got in a big fight with another guy...I picked him up and was hanging him over the tier. Just as I was about to drop him, I remembered what you said and took a breath. And it stopped me, so I put the guy down. He was so shocked he ran off, and I was kinda shocked, too. You were right about that breath stuff!"

YOUR BREATH IS YOUR ALLY. USE IT.

PRACTICE TIPS

TRY IT!

Be willing to try it. You'll only know it works if you give it a shot. Experiment with the breath! Start slow, 5 or 10 minutes a day. Just try to keep it regular.

RESISTANCE

Feeling resistance to meditation practice is normal. Sometimes, meditating is the last thing we would like to be doing. It may seem too difficult or boring. It sometimes feels like it's not working. Thoughts that you're a "bad meditator" might pop up. Meditation is not a quick fix and can easily fall to the bottom of the daily 'to do' list. We may believe that we don't have time for it. We can all come up with good excuses to not meditate.

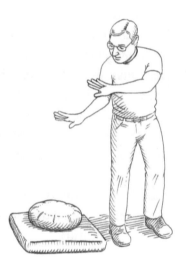

Resistance is normal because human beings are hardwired for comfort and meditation is not comfortable. On the other hand, everyone knows that better habits mean better results. Resistance is just another thought; don't let it dominate your life. Meditation is mind training that takes work, and going beyond resistance is part of the practice sometimes. You can do it!

I'M TOO EMOTIONAL TO SIT STILL!

Don't avoid practice when you are agitated or emotional. It may seem difficult, but these are the times when meditation helps.

N.B.D (NO BIG DEAL)

Agitation, boredom, sleepiness, fantasies, emotions (anger, depression, anxiety, etc.), are all things that can come up during meditation. As our minds begin to slow down and be less distracted, we might become more aware of our thoughts. Don't get swept away-thoughts are just thoughts. Let them happen, and let them pass like birds in the sky. Return to the breath, over and over. Doing this trains our minds to sit peacefully with whatever comes up in life, inside or outside the mind.

DO I NEED A SPECIAL CUSHION OR QUIET PLACE TO MEDITATE?

A meditation cushion and a quiet place to meditate is nice, but life doesn't always work out like that. Meditation is a portable tool; no special place or gear is needed to meditate. All we need is the breath which is always with us.

MINDFULNESS EXERCISE

Stop for a minute and focus your attention outside yourself.
Answer these questions:

I see _____

I hear_____

I smell_____

I feel_____

WALKING MEDITATION

When I walk the mind
will wander.
With each sound the
mind returns.
With each breath the
heart is open.
With each step I touch
this earth.
~ Thich Nhat Hahn

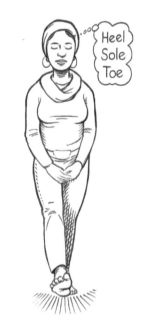

We might spend a good part of our lives on the go. Walking meditation is a way to practice mindfulness while we're moving. During walking meditation we put our attention on our feet rather than our breath. When you notice you are thinking or distracted, simply bring your attention back to the feet and their movement.

You don't need to look at your feet—simply notice how the feet feel, one step at a time: heel, sole, toe; heel, sole, toe. Pay attention to how it feels when the foot touches the ground. Feel each step. Keep your posture upright, alert, and relaxed. You can hold your hands at your sides, or clasped in front of you. Keep your eyes open, cast down, and slightly ahead. Experiment with how fast you walk and find the pace where you feel most present and aware.

You are here, walking on the earth. It's good to be alive!

2. WHO AM I?

TRANSFORMING LIMITING CORE BELIEFS

How would you answer the question, "Who Am I?"

How would you describe yourself if someone asked you?

Who are you? Are you words, roles, labels, or descriptions? Who are you beyond the words? What is your true self? Are you ever afraid or unwilling to show who you really are and end up showing a false mask to the world? What would it be like to drop the mask and just be yourself?

There are probably many things about ourselves that we are proud of, and some things we aren't. Beyond what we might like or not like about ourselves, there is a true self underneath it all we can always trust.

Meditation is a tool that will help you slow down and get in touch with your true self.

LIMITING CORE BELIEFS

"Limiting core beliefs" are negative beliefs we may have about others and ourselves. We might not even know we have them because they often operate under the level of our awareness. These beliefs can make a big impact on our lives because they drive our attitudes, thoughts, feelings, impulses, and behaviors.

EXAMPLES:
I'm not good enough. I don't matter/I'm
not important.
I might get hurt. I might hurt somebody.
I don't deserve it. I'm a bad person.
I can't do it. I'm going to fail.
There's not enough time/money, etc.
I'm scared. I'm stupid.
I'm not good looking enough.
Nobody loves me/I'm not lovable.
I can't trust people.
The world is a scary, dangerous place.

It's not that these core beliefs are "bad," but they can limit our ability to show our talents and intelligence in ways that could bring us happiness.

Sometimes we might hide behind these beliefs as if they were a shield or armor. We can get really caught up in being so 'tough' that it keeps us distant from other people--even the one's we want to be close with.

When we become aware of these limiting beliefs, we can see them for what they are. We can have some humor about them. We can then question them and ask "Is it really true?" "Is this really me?" "Do these beliefs actually serve me?"

If we closely take a look at them, we can see that these beliefs are not even necessarily real. They are just like clothes we put on, and we can actually choose to take them off and wear something else.

Dropping the masks we hide behind might even create freedom in our lives.

EXERCISE:

YOUR LIMITING BELIEFS

Write five of your limiting beliefs or unhealthy identities (i.e. "I am a loser," "I am not good enough," "I am an addict," or, "I'm a bad father/mother," or, "It's all hopeless"). Keep it short:

_____

_____

_____

_____

_____

Now, sit for a minute and try to feel what it would be like if none of these things were you anymore. Who would you be without them? Under all these labels can you glimpse your true self? Without these limiting beliefs . . . Who are You?

What is the impact of your limiting beliefs on others, your family, your kids, your friends? Your whole life? Are you more than just a label or identity? If so, who are you? [1]

---

[1] The "Who Am I?" exercise is adapted from the Alternatives to Violence Project Manual: Basic Course, Revised 2002.

YOUR LIBERATING BELIEFS

Now, come up with five healthy identities or beliefs you have about yourself and list them below. Examples: "loving mother" "good father" "artist" "student" "kind" "funny" "thoughtful" "I can do it!".

_____

_____

_____

_____

_____

Take a moment and think about these identities. Imagine the positive impact these particular roles or beliefs have on your life, family and friends. Feel how this "healthy you" liberates you. You don't need to struggle or change anything about who you truly are. There is nothing wrong with you! Realizing this is true liberation.

"In the 'Who Am I?' class, we wrote five things about who we are. Sometimes I think I'm not good enough, or that I'm worthless. Doing this exercise made me realize I'm not worthless. I'm a good person. I'm a good listener and a loving, helpful, kind daughter, auntie and sister!"
Participant, Path of Freedom Class

SELF WORTH

In contrast to the message "There is something wrong with me" is the reality of our own true self worth. Underneath all of our identities, habits, patterns, roles and behaviors, there is a place in us that is good and whole and worthy. We've all experienced our basic human worth, even if just for a few seconds. Any time your mind stops spinning for a moment (example: seeing a baby smile, watching a beautiful sunset, having a big laugh, doing something creative, cooking a delicious meal) you briefly step out of your busy mind and connect to your own humanness. For that moment there is a deep feeling that "I am okay; life is okay, and all is good —including me."

Many people, even those who seem successful, live their whole lives with an uneasy feeling that they are not okay. This feeling often gets confirmed over and over again by family members, communities, and even whole societies. Through meditation practice, we can experience our own self worth. Through connecting with our own worth, we experience peace, confidence, and relaxation.

This doesn't mean we won't have struggles, issues and problems, but meditation is a great support for working with all of these. When we experience even a small taste of things being basically okay and good no matter what's going on, we can begin to live with more confidence and less fear. It's when we don't feel anything is good or okay, that we will struggle with problems and think that's all life is. Experiencing our own self worth is true freedom. Meditation will help us get there.

BE HERE NOW

Sometimes people think meditation is a religious activity that needs to be done with crossed legs, seated on a special cushion, and with incense and candles burning.

While it can be a spiritual activity, it can also be simply stopping, relaxing, and being present, right here and now.

BE
HERE
NOW

Stop and be here now. Close your eyes and find the still, quiet place inside. It's there, always waiting for you to connect. When was the last time you just stopped and relaxed for just one minute?

TRY THIS ONE-MINUTE MEDITATION:

Stop reading and put your attention on your breath. Simply sit and be with yourself. Be here now. Feel your breath as it flows in and out of your body. Breathe naturally and just feel. After a minute, simply relax the attention on your breath and look around the room.

one minute...

Was it easy? Was your mind racing? Try this over and over during the day. Even one minute of meditation can be a great 'reset' button. Give it a chance to work for you over time. Build your meditation muscles, and deepen your ability to Be Here Now-relaxed and free.

"Be careful what you pretend to be,
because you are what you pretend to be."

Kurt Vonnegut, Writer

3. CHANGE

INSIDE OUT, OUTSIDE IN

How do we go about making real change in our life?

EXERCISE:

Think about it for a few minutes: do you want changes in your life? If your answer is yes, try this:

First, sit quietly and think about what you'd like to change. Would you like to quit smoking? Practice Meditation daily? Eat better? Lose weight? Get in shape? Stop being angry or depressed? Whatever it is, think about it, and notice any feelings that come up. Do you have confidence that you can change? Or do thoughts come up telling you that you can't change? Notice your thoughts and feelings.

Now take a few deep breaths, relax and clear your mind as best you can. Imagine sitting with a friend, at some point in the future. You are telling them about the change you've made in your life and how you did it. Now write these changes down.

"You change for two reasons. Either you learn enough that you want to, or you've been hurt enough that you have to."

Anonymous

OBSTACLES TO CHANGE

Even when we truly want change, making it real and lasting can be difficult for many reasons:

THE POWER OF HABIT

Conditioning and habits are wired into the brain. When we repeat thoughts and react to them with the same emotions and actions over and over, we are laying down grooves in our brain's wiring (called neural pathways or networks). So every time we feel uncomfortable and unconsciously reach for that cigarette or cookie or bottle of beer-we are getting more stuck in a habit groove. When we make a different choice in these habitual moments, such as exercising or meditating instead, we can start to develop new habits (ones with better results!).

Meditation is helpful to rewire habits. The more you meditate, the more conscious you will become of habitual reactions that you were not previously aware of. When we become more aware, we have the ability to make better choices and develop healthier habits. By hijacking our old habits and replacing them with healthier ones, we weaken the strength of these old ways, and program more positive grooves in our brain.

"If you don't like something, change it.
If you can't change it, change your attitude."
Maya Angelou, Writer

FEAR OF CHANGE

Change brings up uncertainty. On the simplest level, change can be difficult because stepping into the future and leaving behind what's familiar is hard. We might be anxious because of fearful thoughts that say, "Change could make things worse!" Many people love the familiar, even if it's not so great. These thoughts undermine and sabotage our efforts. This is perhaps due to an unconscious or even conscious desire to stay in our comfort zone no matter how harmful it is.

FEAR OF SHAME

We've all probably had experiences that left us feeling ashamed. No matter how loving our upbringing may have been, the basic message is: conform or experience shame. Even if our parents delivered that message in a kind way, the message is still there. And for many of us the delivery wasn't so kind, whether that was intended or not. Change involves risk and the possibility of failure. Most of us do not want to fail because we relate failure with shame, which again creates more fear around change. For those with less confidence in their own basic goodness, the possibilities of change become even scarier.

ROMANTIC IDEALISM

We might have a notion that our approach to life is completely justified. We may think our stance is the "right" stance, or even a heroic response to everything that is wrong or hypocritical about

the system. We could even romanticize the idea of being the outlaw, the pirate, or the rebel, which may reinforce destructive and/or criminal behavior patterns that ultimately damage our life. This can be an obstacle to change.

ILLUSION OF SUCCESS

We might think we're successful when we're actually not. We might think we have been a good parent, when in reality we have been operating selfishly without concern for our children. We may think we have been financially successful when our success is really a "House of Cards," that could fall apart any day. We might feel we've been a successful criminal, even as we sit in jail blaming our arrest on others. This illusion of success, and the denial on which it is built, can be a serious obstacle to change.

BEING RIGHT

A lot of people have a strong attachment to being right. The less self-confidence we have, the more attached we are to being right. In some ways, changing involves admitting that we're wrong and that our way didn't work. Not being able to take this step of admitting we are wrong, and ignoring that our approach to life isn't working, can be a huge obstacle to change.

SELF-SABOTAGING LIFE SCRIPTS

These 'scripts' are ideas and beliefs that got conditioned into us during childhood. As a kid, you might have encountered a defining moment. This moment was a powerful experience where you felt unsafe. You have gotten the message that it wasn't okay to be who you are. You might have felt ashamed, or punished, or just simply scared. For example, someone might have told you "You are a bad kid!" When that happened, you began to build a story around your so-called 'badness.' This story became a script for a play or movie in which you are the lead actor: the 'bad person.' You have been playing that role throughout life, finding people who will play all the roles in your script. Playing this same role over and over can lead to the same unwanted results until something causes you to wake up and see that you are not a bad person! The key is to become aware of our own self-sabotaging scripts since they don't serve us. Then we can begin to drop the script, quit believing that old, tiresome story, and make new choices.

Take a moment to reflect: have you ever been tripped up by one of these obstacles to change? Is there a change you have made already where you were able to overcome one of these obstacles? What helped you to get beyond your self-sabotaging scripts?

CHANGE FROM THE INSIDE OUT

Through the practice of mindfulness, we can develop a different way of looking at change. Changing from the "inside out" means we develop the skills of self-awareness and self-reflection. We can then choose to change how we think about things, rather than expecting the world to change for us.

BECOMING MINDFUL

Through practicing meditation we will begin to self-reflect and see clearly some of the sad stories we might have carried for a long time, many of which are connected to real, and often painful, past events. This can be difficult, yet there are benefits to seeing these stories. You can see more easily how your limiting beliefs have been driving you and you can choose to get back in the drivers seat. Mindfulness will support this process. Over time, these stories will become less useful as we outgrow them.

We will then see that life holds more for us than simply replaying all our past hurtful stories over and over. We can change the negative beliefs we have about others and ourselves, and heal the shame and trauma that we've kept silently inside. Meditation will help us connect deeply with the best parts of ourself. It allows us to become confident in who we are—a good person with good heart who has potential--no matter what challenges we face.

INCREASING AWARENESS OF PAIN (CONSEQUENCES)
A first step in being able to create change is to become vividly aware of our pain, anxiety or discomfort. We shift out of denial and/or running from our pain and take a look at it--face it head on. We may even begin to realize pain is often a consequence of our own behavior. This awareness may be the primary thing that will shift us out of denial as well as the cocoon of old patterns that create suffering. Something needs to trigger some kind of motivation for us to change, and generally it is discomfort or pain. It is either discomfort with the way things are, or the discomfort of wishing things could be different.

DEVELOPING AWARENESS OF IMPACT (EMPATHY)
Becoming aware of our impact on others can also motivate change. When we are too wrapped up in ourself, we might behave in ways that harm others and are clueless about it. People will let us know if we are negatively impacting them. Listen to their feedback-it can be a powerful motivator to change-not out of shame—but to be a caring person treating others as you would like to be treated.

CONFIDENCE
Finding confidence in our own worth and goodness will help dissolve a lot of our negative limiting core beliefs. Over time, practicing meditation will help us develop confidence. Through training and relaxing our minds in meditation, we can experience a deep, satisfying peace with who we are. The more confidence we develop in our own worth, the more our fear will not rule, and love and kindness will shine through.

REFRAMING NEGATIVE THINKING

Reframing is changing negativity into perspectives that will be more helpful. Often negative thinking is 'black and white,' meaning it's solid thinking that things are either 'this way' or 'that way.' Reframing helps us open up to new ways of seeing things. Instead of jumping to negative conclusions in difficult circumstances, we can stop and work with reframing our perspective. Difficult experiences can be challenging, yet they can also be opportunities for us to grow, learn, and become stronger. By reframing we can see things less as heavy problems that we have to live with and more as challenges we can tackle and learn from.

EXAMPLES OF REFRAMING:

EXAMPLE: "I can't trust anyone!"
REFRAME: "I have some people I can really depend on and trust."
EXAMPLE: "Everyone around here is a criminal or just weird, so I refuse to get to know anyone!"
REFRAME: There are some people in my world that I can learn a lot from about how to get through difficult situations.

STATE SHIFTING EMOTIONAL TRIGGERS

State shifting involves using tools to shift our state of mind from agitation and overwhelm to a state where we are better able to think and positively respond. For example, when you are angry and count to ten, or take ten deep breaths before doing or saying anything, this will help you calm down and make better decisions. You shift your 'state' by doing this. In terms of biology, we are shifting from a "Fight, Flight or Freeze" reaction to more clear and helpful thinking. Meditation is a powerful form of state shifting. Whenever you notice you are in a 'Fight Flight or Freeze' mode, take several long deep breaths. Does it shift your state of mind?

BUILDING RESILIENCE

Resilience is an internal strength that gives us the ability to cope with stress and anxiety. It is defined in Webster's Dictionary as "The power or ability to return to the original position after being bent or stretched." Through meditation practice we can develop greater resilience in working with difficult emotions and stressors.

Resilience is about having the ability to recover quickly from being 'bent out of shape' by depressing, "crazy-making," or worrisome life events. It allows us to bounce back more quickly to a good place in our heads and hearts. Being resilient helps us deal with stress better and to cope more skillfully with anything life throws at us.

EXPERIMENT: CHANGING HABITS

Lots of scientific research has been done on how habits develop and how to change them. Most agree that repetition is the key to developing good and bad habits.

THE "40 DAY" PLAN: Use this plan for any negative habit you would like to change, or positive habit you would like to develop. Try it with meditation!

40 DAYS: Practice meditation every day for 40 days. Decide how much time you want to do each day (5, 10, 20 minutes, etc). Pick a time and stick with it. Complete 40 straight days. This will help establish meditation as a positive habit.

90 DAYS: Practice every day for 90 days straight. This will establish a way to work with your mind and will change you in a deeper way. As with building any habit, meditation will become part of your daily life, like brushing your teeth. Teeth brushing is a well-established habit for most people. If you forget to brush your teeth, you will notice it. After 90 days straight, meditation will be easy to remember and you'll want to do it daily.

120 DAYS: Practice every day for 120 days straight. This will further confirm the new habit. The positive benefits of meditation will weave permanently into your brain.

1000 DAYS: Practice every day for 1000 days straight. This will bring you much deeper mastery of meditation practice. No matter what the challenge, you will remember to call on this firmly planted habit (meditation) to serve you.

By doing a 40, 90, 120 or 1000 practice, you can rewire your chain reactions and develop deep habits that serve you.

"The moment one gives close attention to anything, even a blade of grass, it becomes a mysterious, awesome, indescribably magnificent world in itself."

Henry Miller, Writer

CHANGE FROM THE OUTSIDE IN

Our thoughts, attitudes, and feelings drive our behaviors and result in consequences (inside-out). For example, if we are stressed, we are more likely to be irritated and lash out and then suffer the results. It is also true that behaviors affect our mind states. As in: the more I lash out the more cranky I feel. So, another approach to change (outside-in) is to intentionally practice behaviors that support positive mind states. For example, we might have the experience that cleaning our room results in pleasant feelings. Positive behavior (outside) leads to positive feelings (inside).

Here are some things to do that support positive change to stick:

BEING MINDFUL

BODY: Sitting still in the posture of meditation, will support a positive mind state and a healthy body. Tracking your physical needs (thirst, hunger, tiredness, etc.) is important because when we are hungry or tired, we become less resilient.

SPEECH: Being mindful of your words and their effect on others helps you say things that won't create hostility or defense in others. Not having to deal with blow-back will probably make you feel better.

ACTIONS: Being mindful of actions allows you to be more conscious of what you are doing. Example: Being mindless when driving a car can get you into some serious trouble! Or, when trying to lose weight, you can mindlessly gulp up an entire bag of chips without even knowing it.

KEEPING IT SIMPLE

The acronym KISS (Keep It Simple Stupid) is often used in 12-step recovery programs. Change is difficult. Our natural way might be to follow the path of least resistance. If we bite off too much when trying to change, we might be setting ourself up for failure. Start small; don't try to change it all at once-set yourself up for success!

Example: Meditating two hours a day might be a hard goal to keep up. Just 10-20 minutes a day will change your life if you are consistent. Keep it simple!

BECOME A "PRACTITIONER"

"Practice makes perfect" is a wise statement. One of the ways we learn anything is through repetition. In meditation circles, meditation is often called "practice." People who practice meditation are known as 'practitioners.' In reality, we are all always practicing something. The question is--what are you practicing? We might spend a great deal of your time unconsciously practicing all sorts of things. We might practice spacing out or being a workaholic or

any number of things that are basically just unconscious habits. These habits are always on the job, 24/7. The good news is that conscious practice is much more effective to create good things in your life than unconscious practice. Try replacing one 'bad' habit a month with something more positive. Example: replace 20 minutes of TV "practice" with 20 minutes of exercise or yoga practice. Do you notice a difference?

CHANGE TALK

The amount of time we spend talking about change has a direct effect on change actually happening. Research has shown that change talk leads to change. By engaging in change talk, we move from not thinking about change or being in denial, to thinking about how and what we might want to change-which is a necessary step in making actual change.[2]

"The only way to make sense out of change is to plunge into it, move with it, and join the dance."

Alan Watts, Writer

---

2 Stages of Change Theory, Prochaska, J.O. and DiClemente C.C.,1986.

SUSTAINING THE CHANGE-AVOIDING RELAPSE

ENVIRONMENT

We all know our environment impacts our behaviors. If we have a sweet tooth and want to lose weight and then spend our time in a place where everyone is eating lots of sweets and desserts, this is clearly a setup for failure. We cannot control everything in our environment, and we may have limited choices when it comes to our living situations; but nonetheless, we do have choices. How can you exercise choice to create an environment that's supportive of the changes you want to make?

COMMUNITY

For many years, humans have formed communities of practice designed to encourage and support positive change. Human beings are social animals. Connection with others is a basic human need. We learn through imitation and social reinforcement. Being included in a support group can be a powerful motivator toward healthier behavior. In 12-Step recovery programs we hear things like, "If you want recovery, hang with the winners," and you hear about the importance of community and attending meetings (90 meetings in 90 days) is at the very heart of the recovery (change) process. How can you find or create a supportive community of practice that shares your vision for positive change? How can this POF class or book help you create a positive community of practice? Are you still engaged in negative communities of practice? If so, find a more positive group to hang with or start one yourself!

CELEBRATE!

Celebrating our success creating change, however small, helps to sustain the change. Getting together with friends to celebrate and laugh is good medicine. Humorist Arnold Glasow said: "Laughter is a tranquilizer with no side effects." Give yourself a "change reward"-celebrate!

SUSTAINING CHANGE

Change is difficult. Relapsing and backsliding happens. It can be tempting to beat ourself up about it and use it as an excuse to give up or become hopeless. Try looking at things another way. See it as an opportunity to refresh your commitment, deepen your practice, be humble, and better understand how falling off the wagon happens. Maybe it's time to look at boundaries—the ability to say "No" to others (or ourselves). Sometimes saying "No" is saying "Yes" to change. The key is to never give up, pick yourself up, dust yourself off, and get back on the horse.

CHANGE + YOUR BRAIN
-A CLOSER LOOK AT NEURAL NETWORKS

Our brains have a network of neural pathways made up of nerve cells that connect the logical, emotional and instinctual networks of the brain. When we have an emotional experience and react to it in a habitual way, our nerve cells get stimulated over and over and "neurons that fire together wire together." This clever phrase was first used in 1949 by Donald Hebb, a Canadian neuropsychologist. Hebb's words remind us that every experience,

thought, feeling, and physical sensation triggers thousands of neurons, which form a neural network. This repetition creates a stronger and deeper neural pathway in the brain, which can help us react in better ways in similar situations.

Say you get in an argument and you feel angry. You react by yelling or pushing someone. If there is no time or space between your emotion and your reaction then you are strengthening the particular pathway that will lead you, again and again, to react when you are angry by yelling or pushing. In effect, your brain will be programmed to always react with anger.

THE ART OF STOPPING: PART ONE

The bad news is that your brain is programmed by past experiences, choices, and actions. This is why it seems so hard to change habits. The good news is that you can change the programming and start to rewire your brain by stopping, becoming aware, and making healthier choices. Most of us just haven't worked much with the art of stopping. Meditation is all about this.

When we stop, and don't make the same habitual choice each time an emotion comes up, our nerve pathways will shrivel, getting weaker. We can then have a chance to make a different choice on how we react.

To perfect the art of stopping each time you feel triggered to react try something different, such as: slow down, take a few breaths, go for a walk, talk to a friend, write in a journal, write a poem, do deep breathing, exercise, meditate, do yoga, sing, dance, stare at the sky —anything that cuts the speed or your programmed reaction. This will short-circuit the habit by rewiring your brain. This process of re-wiring is gradual and will take longer if habits are deep. However, if we don't start to change these habitual reactions now, nothing in our life will change and we will, in effect, be programmed or wired to repeat mistakes over and over.

"I know if I go out there and don't change I'll just end up back here — the Path of Freedom is already helping me change."
Participant, POF Prison Class

BREATH COUNTING

Try "Breath Counting" meditation at least once a day for five minutes every day this week.

Sit or lie down in a comfortable position with your spine straight. Take a deep belly breath. Pause before you exhale. When you exhale, count "one" silently. As you continue to inhale and exhale, count each exhalation "two"..."three"..."four."
When you reach four, begin again with "one."
Continue counting your exhales in sets of four, for five to ten minutes. Watch your breath slow, your body relax, and your mind calm.

Use this meditation tool to calm yourself any time your mind is agitated or racing with thoughts. If your mind drifts, no big deal—simply refocus on your breath and count each out breath..."one"..."two" ..."three"..."four".

"Meditation doesn't change life. Life remains as fragile and unpredictable as ever. Meditation changes the heart's capacity to accept life as it is. It teaches the us to be more accepting, not by beating it into submission, but by making it clear that acceptance is a great choice."
Sylvia Boorstein, Author

SELF-REFLECTIONS ON CHANGE

Contemplate the following:

- What do I want to change?
- Who might support me with feedback?
- What is 'not changing' costing me?
- What are the rewards and benefits of change?
- What obstacles derail my attempts to change?
- What is my change plan...what steps can I take?
- Who will hold me accountable?
- Where can I find a positive community of practice?
- What is my relapse strategy?
- How will I celebrate when the change occurs?
- How can I make my environment supportive?

4. HOLDING YOUR SEAT

MANAGING EMOTIONAL TRIGGERS

The expression 'Hold Your Seat' comes from a type of horseback riding called dressage. In dressage, the rider keeps their seat firmly in the saddle as the horse moves. Practicing meditation is all about holding your seat, regardless of whatever situations happen in your life. We can learn to hold our seat calmly and peacefully, even in the most intense moments: during difficult emotions, strong desires, overwhelming needs, or conflicts. Being able to hold your seat through chaos is a powerful skill.

Learning to hold your seat through the intensely hot fire of tough situations builds emotional intelligence. Emotional Intelligence is defined as skill in managing emotions and feelings. Being emotionally intelligent is a valuable talent that will serve you all of your days.

Without mindfulness and emotional intelligence, your situation could be like a rider who has fallen off the saddle with one foot still stuck in the stirrup. As the horse (our thoughts, feelings, and impulses) gallops off down the road, you are dragged along with your head banging on the ground, hitting every rock and obstacle on the path.

The practice of meditation trains us to hold our seat and ride the energy of our minds with grace and skill. By practicing regularly, we will learn to hold our seat more and more.

HOLDING YOUR SEAT IS:

- Remaining calm and non-reactive when emotionally triggered.
- Learning to recognize when we are triggered and using our breath and our posture to shift to a calm state of mind.
- Being peaceful during meditation practice.

THE ART OF STOPPING: PART TWO

History is filled with a long, long list of folks who never learned the Art of Stopping. This has been the cause of wars, conflicts, and countless day-to-day dramas and upsets throughout time. There is real benefit to learning a different way, and interrupting patterns of reactivity and conflict.

Sometimes all you need is to put on the brakes before you end up in a giant crash of emotional reactivity. Learning how to just simply STOP when triggered might be one of the most important things you could learn in life. This one technique alone—if you master it—can change your life completely.

When triggered-don't act. Sounds simple, but it takes practice to actually remember in the heat of the moment.

How do you know when you are triggered? Check your body and mind. Are you agitated? Are you breathing rapidly, feeling tense or upset? Are your thoughts racing or looping over and over on the same subject? Just think of the word 'trigger' itself—it implies that you are on the edge, waiting to pull the trigger and then away you go—straight into the reality of unwanted consequences. Listen to your own voice, it generally can give you a clue when you are wound up and tense and ready to fly off the handle with someone. When all this is happening, there is one effective solution that works

SIMPLY STOP AND DO NOTHING.

PERFECTING THE ART OF STOPPING

TIP #1: IF TRIGGERED-DON'T ACT-DON'T SPEAK

Remember the kinds of results you have gotten in the past when you either acted or spoke when triggered. Generally it's not a pretty sight. Someone said once that "Anger=short term gain, long term loss." When you don't stop, harm is caused, problems are created, and messes are made. Stop the pattern by simply stopping. Even if you aren't immediately sure what to do, just STOP.

STOP AND THINK!

Remember a time when you were triggered and acted without thinking. What happened?

TIP #2: NAME IT

This may sound obvious, but a lot of the times when we are triggered we are so wrapped up in our emotional reaction, we can barely recognize that we are triggered. If you get a glimpse that you are---Name It. Say it out loud or silently to yourself, "I'm Triggered!" This will help to slow the reactivity down a bit.

TIP # 3: MAKE SPACE

Step away from the situation. Step back. Get some fresh air. If for some reason you can't physically move away, and feel crowded in by triggery situations—take some deep breaths and stay still. This will help to create some space in your thoughts.

TIP #4: USE YOUR RESOURCES TOOLKIT

Do whatever it takes to calm down and resource yourself, drawing on the internal tools you have to shift your state of mind. Resourcing might involve: counting to ten, taking some deep breaths, meditating, doing yoga, walking, running, reading a book, or even putting a goldfish bowl on your head and dancing around...in other words do whatever it takes to shift your state of mind from the story that is triggering your mind to lose control.

AFTER YOU HAVE CALMED DOWN:

TIP #5: ID'ING YOUR OWN PARTICULAR TRIGGERS

Train yourself to recognize your own triggers and it will be easier to work with them. You know what they are, you've lived with them your whole life. Be aware and as one starts to appear, put on the brakes! Don't make this just a mental exercise...it's also important to be aware of any habitual physical sensations that arise when you are triggered (clenched jaw, stomach churning, tight shoulders, shaking, etc).

TIP #6: OWN IT: USE "I" STATEMENTS TO MOVE FROM PROJECTION TO REFLECTION

This means moving from blaming our feelings and reactions on something outside ourselves to owning them. Use "I" statements (in your mind and even out loud) to identify and own your feelings (I'm feeling overwhelmed, frustrated, or annoyed) and to identify and own underlying needs (I'm feeling frustrated because I need: space, help, respect, to know that I matter, etc.).

TIP #7: RESPOND-ONLY

After you are no longer triggered, you can speak to the situation from a calm place. You will be better at responding to tough situations when holding your seat with calm, respect, and stillness.

"If someone or something triggers me in a bad way I stop and think before reacting. Mindfulness this week was a big help!"
Participant, POF Prison Class

BEING AN ADULT

At some point in your life someone might have said to you "Act like an adult!" But what does that really mean? An Adult is able to resource themselves when triggered, and is able to calmly and skillfully consider the best course of action. In the mindset of being an Adult we respond, as opposed to react, to whatever happens.

Example: your roommate says "You're such a jerk you always take my stuff without asking!"

Example (reacting): "You're the jerk! And don't talk to me like that!"

Example (responding): Take a deep breath. You feel your irritation coming up. Think back to what they are talking about. Oh yeah, They also borrowed your toothpaste. You don't like their tone, but you know that they aren't going to react well to you pointing that out now. Probably better just to apologize and get on with your day. "Woah, I'm sorry, you're right. I shouldn't take your things without asking. I won't do it again."

Learning how to be an Adult (especially when triggered) is another valuable skill. When we are not holding our seat as an Adult, we might might act in not such great ways that we aren't even aware of. These are likely behaviors and ways of reacting that we learned in the past, often when we were very young.

These behaviors are linked to the dysfunctional side of two other mindsets: the "Parent" and "The Child." The Parent/Adult/Child ego state model comes from a psychological model called Transactional Analysis developed by Dr. Eric Berne.[3]

"It's not so much what happens, as it is how we are with ourselves regardless of what happens, that makes the difference in our lives."
Cheri Huber, Zen Teacher

[3] Transactional Analysis was developed by psychiatrist Eric Berne in the 1950s and was first published in the book Transactional Analysis in Psychotherapy (Secaucus, NJ: Castle, 1961).

THE PARENT:

The Parent mindset includes all the behaviors that were programmed (conditioned) into you from your parents and other adults or authority figures in your childhood. When you are acting from the Adult mindset you will exhibit the qualities of the "Healthy Parent." When you are unconsciously acting out, you can slip into the learned behavior of the "Dysfunctional Parent."

HEALTHY PARENT:

Nurturing

Protecting

Mentoring

Supporting

DYSFUNCTIONAL (NOT-SO-HEALTHY) PARENT:

Judgemental

Critical

Domineering

Controlling

Blaming

THE CHILD:

The "Child" mindset also includes healthy and dysfunctional aspects. The more dysfunctional qualities of "The Child" often show up when we are feeling emotionally triggered by something or someone.

HEALTHY CHILD:

Playful
Creative
Spontaneous
Curious
Adventurous
Open

DYSFUNCTIONAL CHILD:

Reactive

Needy

Manipulative

Whining, complaining

"Throwing a tantrum"

Acting out

What does this have to do with Holding Your Seat? When emotionally triggered, most people immediately shift into the dysfunctional aspects of either the Parent (blaming) or the Child (complaining).

With mindfulness, one can learn to shift into the Adult when triggered, unhooking yourself from the dysfunctional Parent or Child mindsets. You can learn to recognize these behaviors for what they are: reactive behaviors that were programmed and conditioned into you when you were young. Learning to hold your seat in the Adult mindset is not always easy. You've had a lifetime to practice reactivity, so responding to situations in a less reactive way can feel difficult at first. It will take practice to condition a new way of responding. The more you practice, the more you will transform how you respond which will lead to better results.

THE ADULT=
Thoughts, feelings & behaviors grounded in the present.

STEPS:
A simple way to get into the Adult is to
• Become present,
• Sit up straight, and
• Take a few deep breaths.

Taking these steps will give you time to shift into your adult where you have access to all the best parts of yourself. When you are firmly rooted in your Adult mindset, you have more access to the healthy qualities of the Parent mindset (nurturing, supportive) and the healthy qualities of the Child (playful, creative, joyful). You can begin to live your life grounded in the present (rather than the past or future) and make choices that actually make your life and the lives of your own friends and family better.

All the meditations in this book are designed to help you Hold Your Seat and Be an Adult in triggering situations. If you practice these regularly (when you are not triggered), you will notice a difference in how you respond when you do get triggered. Over time you will be amazed by your ability to stay grounded and centered when upsetting things happen, even things that used to make you totally lose your cool

THE GAP

Concentration camp survivor Viktor Frankl said, "Between stimulus and response, there is a space. In that space lies our freedom and power to choose our response."

In meditation we call that place of freedom 'The Gap.' This gap is the space between thoughts and actions, the place where you have freedom to choose better results. The practice of meditation also leads to developing patience. Patience allows you to experience the gap which is only found in the present moment, here and now.

TREE MEDITATION:

Another way to imagine holding your seat is to envision yourself as a tree in the wind. Read this poem as a short meditation, visualizing yourself as a dignified tree in the forest.

Like an ancient tree in the forest
Standing tall and powerful
I'm grounded and strong
My deep roots supporting me

Wild winds, I dance and sway
Fierce winds blowing, don't break me
Whatever sun, rains, or thunder appears
My steady center stays rooted on the earth

Holding my Seat, bearing witness
I remain strong—as chaos comes and goes
Vast sky above
Vast energy in space
Strength of the earth below
Winds blowing through space
My human dignity remains.

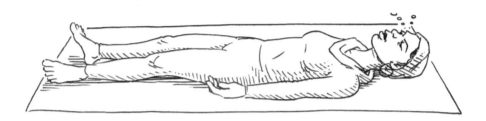

DEEP BELLY BREATH MEDITATION

This meditation can be done at night in your bed or anytime you can lie down for a few minutes. Try to practice it each day this week for at least 10 minutes.

Lie down on your back. Put both of your hands on your belly. Breathe in deeply through your nose. Let your belly expand as far as it can. Next, exhale through your mouth. Let out a quiet sigh as you exhale.

Feel your face, your jaw, your shoulders, and your entire body relax as you exhale. Breathe deeply into your belly nine times. With each exhale, feel your body relax even more. Let all the tension in your body melt into the floor or bed under you.

It's ok if you become so relaxed that you fall asleep.
Breathe deep... relax.

5. WORKING WITH PAIN + ANXIETY

Everyone on the planet has felt pain—either in the body (physical) or in the feelings (emotional). There are many ways to deal with pain – including distraction, frustration, and denial. Sometimes when we try to get rid of pain, the pain can get even worse. For example, when we take pain medicine, our bodies become more sensitive to pain, and we need more and more medicine to feel relief. This can lead to wanting to take more and more medicine, which can result in wanting more medicine than the doctor will prescribe. You probably can imagine what happens next. This chapter looks at ways you can deal with pain and anxiety that don't create more pain.

PHYSICAL PAIN can show up in our bodies with sensations such as: stabbing, burning, aching, shooting, itching, tension, constriction,

nausea, etc. With emotional pain we might feel anger, grief, sadness, fear, shame, loss, guilt, etc. For thousands of years people have used mindfulness as a tool to deal with pain and suffering. By using Mindfulness, we are able to focus directly on the energy, sensation, or feeling of the pain. Instead of getting lost in the story and thoughts that surround the pain and we simply feel the actual sensation(s) of our pain without judgment or resistance.

When we use mindfulness to work with our pain, the physical or emotional feeling of the pain might remain, but the stuck energy—that happens when we think about it too much, will begin to break down and go away. While dealing with pain through mindfulness is not a fast fix, it is a more long-lasting way to decrease suffering.

PAIN IS NOT THE SAME AS 'SUFFERING'

Do you respond to pain with fear and resistance—either mental or physical? Mental resistance can look like: looping thoughts, judgments, hopes, wishes, fear, paranoia, etc. In pain we might have thoughts that end up adding to the suffering around the pain. Our body might then react to that resistance by becoming more stressed. Then, on top of the initial pain, we might develop muscle tension, headaches or other stress related health problems. It's not the actual pain that causes suffering, it's the looping thoughts, feelings, and stress.

Addressing our thoughts and stress reactions with mindfulness will help to reduce the suffering aspect of pain. We do this by putting all of our attention on the actual sensations that we are feeling. As you do this, stay with the sensations and boycott any anxious thoughts or stories. There is no way to avoid pain in life—but you can avoid unnecessary suffering.

PAIN AND IMPERMANENCE

Pain can seem very solid and feel like it will last forever. As we practice mindfulness, we will begin to understand the truth of impermanence. Impermanence is the truth that everything is temporary and nothing stays exactly the same forever. Same goes for pain, it's not always the same—it changes. Sensations of pain can shift every few seconds, and definitely over time. Sensations get stronger, weaker, tighter, looser, expand or contract. Pain can shift from moment to moment in its texture or style: burning becomes itching, anger becomes sadness, etc. All pain is energy, and energy shifts and changes continually. Meditation will help you become aware of the impermanence of all things and situations, and helps you see that pain does change; it doesn't stay the same forever.

WHY OUR MINDS BECOME ANXIOUS

Humans are programmed to survive. Anxiety and fearful thoughts developed as one way to protect us as we evolved. They are primal reactions. Humans are programmed to constantly be on the lookout in our environments for what might be dangerous and find what is safe and secure to help with survival. The biology of anxiety might seem difficult to work with now but in the past it has been the key to our survival.

We all know that when bad things happen we remember them, they stick. For example, if a dog once bit you, whenever you are near a dog, no matter how friendly it is, you might feel a little bit of fear. You can have flashes of fear and anxiety over things you have experienced yourself, or things you've heard about happening to others. Sometimes we may even feel fearful of things that were dangers for our ancestors. All this leads to an overload of thinking. Our brains constantly scan the environment, checking to see what is safe, to ensure we will survive the next moment.

COMPONENTS OF ANXIETY

PHYSICAL:

The part of the brain that is activated in sensing danger (the amygdala) sends signals to other parts of the brain. More signals are sent to other areas of the body and adrenaline is released. The adrenaline helps to create the physical and emotional feelings of anxiety and stress. When this primal survival instinct happens frequently, it can cause many of the results of stress in the body such as: nervous system upset, tension, increased blood pressure, a faster heart rate, muscles tensing up, etc. This all occurs before you have any thoughts about the situation. This is important to know: the part of the brain that is activated when you sense danger has recorded the sights and sounds related to past fearful memories, and it then sends the body into "high alert" even before you understand what is happening or why.

MENTAL + EMOTIONAL:

Next our mind begins to have thoughts that add to the reactions of the body and emotions start happening. Sometimes it's the

thoughts that come first, sometimes the emotions come first. The emotions: anxiety, fear, uncertainty, worry, lack of ease, discomfort, frustration, irritation can all tumble together. These emotions are like a tiger, ready to pounce. We might even become fearful of the emotions themselves, and try not to feel them.

ASSESSING ACTUAL RISK

At this point it's helpful to assess actual risk. Assessment is where we decide whether we are actually unsafe. Our physical and emotional reactions have an effect on us so we need to be clear what is actually at stake.

FOR EXAMPLE:

Someone is walking down a street and they hear someone walking behind them quickly. They think: "Someone is behind me! What are they doing!" or "What was that noise?!" or "Are they going to rob me?!" They are on alert and walking faster and faster, hoping to get to their destination before the worst happens.

Another person walks down a street and hears someone behind them, walking quickly. They think, "Someone must be in a rush, I'll step out of the way so they can pass. It's a beautiful, sunny, day. I want to walk slowly and enjoy it."

What's the difference between these two people? Their assessment! Both (or neither) of these assessments might be correct. The important thing to notice here is the thinking involved and the level of anxiety for the first person, compared to the second person. Even a little bit of fear can cause us to go on alert and immediately begin to have anxious thoughts. The most noticeable thing about a mind in fear or anxiety is how it leaps toward a disastrous future. Anxiety is the fear that something terrible might happen and getting totally wrapped up in that fear of the future.

Stop for a moment here: think about something you are anxious about. Notice if you are having thoughts about bad things that might happen in the future. Notice if your mind is creating possible situations that are horrible (or even catastrophic!). In reality, you are just sitting here thinking. We all do this over and over again. Maybe we are wired genetically for worry, maybe not. Genetic wiring is not something you can do much about. What you can do is work with rewiring your brain now to be more relaxed.

Mindfulness works with anxious thoughts by planting us firmly in the now, feeling our feet, feeling the breath, seeing clearly what is happening now (and what isn't!).

In the above example, a person using mindfulness might be able to assess what was really happening--beyond their thoughts. If they notice anxiety, they would be able to manage it. They would then be able to calmly choose the best action possible for the situation. That might mean choosing to go down a different street, or choosing to simply keep walking or even start running. Either way, the person made a choice and they held their seat. Mindfulness is a great antidote to fear and anxiety.

SITTING WITH THE TIGER

How can we use mindfulness to bring relief to the anxiety we experience 'naturally' as a part of our genetic programming? First thing, anxiety can get worse when we try to avoid it. We might think that it would get worse if we don't avoid it, but many people have discovered the opposite. When we give it 'permission' to be here and accept or even welcome it, the symptoms and sensations can weaken. Mindfulness is a tool to work with this. When meditating with anxiety we are in effect 'sitting with the tiger' rather than running from it. Our body will relax when we no longer feel the need to run from danger. If we do nothing but focus with curiosity on the feelings and sensations (not thoughts) of the anxiety, it will begin to dissolve, and the 'tiger' will just be sitting there with us, no longer a threat.

By doing this we change our relationship to anxiety. The sensations of anxiety will relax by simply holding our seat and accepting its energy. Mindfulness practice will allow us to see that it's impossible to hold life, or our fears, still. We can develop true fearlessness (not bravado fearlessness) by simply sitting with fear and accepting it. Life doesn't hold still. When we relax our grip on fear, change happens.

WORKING WITH PANIC

Panic is defined as an overwhelming rush of fear that comes up, sometimes for what seems like no reason. When we feel panic, our heart beats faster and our breathing changes. When we panic, we might hold our breath without knowing it, or begin to gasp. This results in not enough air getting into the lungs. Our body reacts with more rapid, shallow breathing. This is known as hyperventilation.

Hyperventilation is what triggers panic attacks. When someone is having a panic attack, they can feel like they are having a heart attack, or like they can't breathe. Below are some meditations and practices for working with Anxiety and Panic.

MEDITATION FOR ANXIETY: FOCUS ON THE EXHALE

When you notice the first signs of nervousness or panic—when you notice rapid breath or you are having thoughts that you might 'pass out' or 'not be able to breathe' . . . first . . . exhale. Breathe out a large exhale. This is an important step. When you exhale, your lungs will open up and allow a large inhale to follow.

Then, slowly inhale and exhale through your nose. Exhaling through your nose will slow down your breathing and prevent the hyperventilation. If you can't breathe through your nose, inhale through your mouth and then make a large purifying exhale through your mouth.

Take another large exhale. Put one hand on your belly and one on your chest. Inhale through your nose. Count . . . one . . . two . . . three. Pause. Exhale through your mouth. Count . . . one . . . two . . . three . . . four . . .five. Pause.

Your exhale should always be longer than your inhale. This will prevent you from taking quick, gaspy breaths. Do this a few times. Then, increase the slow count to four on the inhale and six on the exhale.

MEDITATION FOR ANXIETY: STRAW BREATH

- Inhale through your nose and exhale as if you are blowing through a straw.
- Rest your tongue on the roof of your mouth during the inhalation so you don't inhale through the 'straw.'
- Fill the the lungs on each inhale, all the way into the belly.
- Then exhale through the imaginary 'straw' fully and slowly.

Practice this for three minutes. This is another technique for exhaling longer than inhaling which activates the 'relaxation' response in your nervous system.

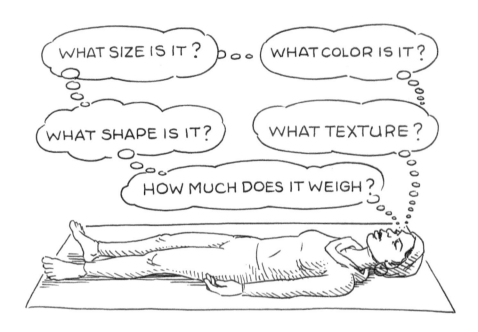

MINDFULNESS MEDITATION FOR PAIN

- Lie down and close your eyes.
- Let your body sink down into whatever you are lying on, allowing it to hold you.
- Choose a place in the body where you feel pain or discomfort.

Imagine you are a witness, or scientist, simply watching the energy of the pain. Look at it with curiosity and interest.

Bring your attention to the pain with focus and intent, and answer the following questions silently:

- What is the size or shape of the painful area?
- How much does it weigh? 1 pound, 5 pounds, 10 pounds?
- What is its texture? Is it rough, sharp, spikey, dull?
- What color is it?
- Does it spread or stay in one place?
- Does it get more intense or less intense?

Watch the pain energy carefully. Notice if it changes—-every time you notice changes in the sensations, even a little bit, allow your body to relax into the space created. Notice what happens.

CROSS BRAIN TRAINING: "CROSS OVERS"

Crossing our arms and/or legs over the center line of our body will help calm us down. This is why sometimes taking a walk is helpful when we are feeling anxious, irritable, or overwhelmed.. "Cross Overs" will help relax us when we're irritated, triggered, or in conflict. For best results, do the following twice each day:

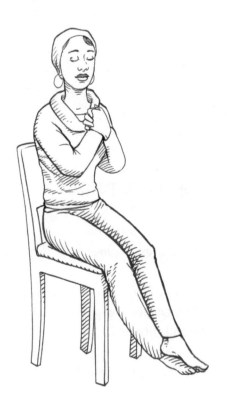

Sit on a chair with legs outstretched. Cross one ankle over the other.

Now stretch your arms forward with the backs of your hands facing one another and your thumbs pointing down.

Then lift one hand over the other (now your palms face one another are touching). Interlock your fingers.

Now roll the locked hands straight down and in toward the body so they eventually come to rest on the chest with your knuckles facing your chin. Sit calmly in this cross over for 3-5 minutes. Focus on the breath. Cross Overs balance the left (logical) and right (emotional) hemispheres of the brain. They allow us to relax, dissolve stress, and see things more clearly. In our prison programs, we often devote a few minutes to Cross Overs, and students report that this helps them calm down. One young man even told me once, "That was the most calm I've ever experienced in my entire life."

Fear ...

Is the path to the dark side.
Fear leads to anger.
Anger leads to hate.
Hate leads to suffering.

Yoda, Star Wars episode
"The Phantom Menace"

MEDITATION: 4,7,8 BREATH

The perfect portable stress antidote!
First, let all of the air out through a long exhale
Close the mouth and place the tongue on roof of the mouth
Breathe in for the count of 4
Hold the breath for the count of 7
Breathe out with a forceful 'whoosh' sound for the count of 8, let all the air out.

Do 4 cycles of this, 2 times a day but don't do more than 4 cycles.

This helps with falling asleep, reducing cravings and anxiety, and impulse control. Do this exercise after you have learned it well, in daily life. For example: someone says something that triggers you...do this practice.

ANXIETY TIP: # 1
GROUND YOURSELF

Grounding can help you when you feel like you have lost control.

Look around you. Name (silently—to yourself):
- 5 things you can see
- 4 things you can touch
- 3 things you can hear
- 2 things you can smell
- 1 thing you can taste

ANXIETY TIP: # 2
REASSURE YOURSELF

Acknowledge your worries, then tell yourself you can handle whatever comes up.

EXAMPLE OF WHAT TO SAY (AND NOT SAY):
NOT HELPFUL: "That's not going to happen and here are the reasons why..."
HELPFUL: "If something real is happening, I have the tools to figure out what to do."

ANXIETY TIP: # 3
REMIND YOURSELF

Panic is unpleasant but it doesn't kill you. You will survive it.

ANXIETY TIP: # 4
DEBUNK CATASTROPHIZING

Catastrophizing is when we have thoughts that are not rational about a situation, believing that it is far worse than it actually is. For instance, you might think that because a family member hasn't called in a while, perhaps they are angry with you and will never speak to you again. Or, as you look into the future, you can only see all of the negative things that you are sure will happen. It's giving things an overblown "negative spin."

Think Chicken Little: "The sky is falling!"

Debunking = "A Reality Check"

EXAMPLES:
- Thinking you are dying or going crazy when panic occurs
- I'll always panic when I drive/fly/end up in court
- I've totally lost control
- I'll always say/do the wrong thing
- This headache must be a brain tumor!!

ANXIETY TIP: # 5
CATCH THE DREAD EARLY

Dread can occur even when nothing is happening. Some of us feel anxiety all the time, and/or we are always on the lookout for the next 'awful thing' that might happen. When you notice that 'dread' feeling occurring, it's the time to get it in check and do some deep breathing. Panic can be nipped in the bud if you practice with the breath when the dread first hits.

"You change your relationship to the pain by opening up to it and paying attention to it. You put out the welcome mat.

Not because you're masochistic, but because the pain is there. You understand as the doctors say, 'learning to live with it,' or, as Buddhists say, 'liberation from the suffering.' If you know the difference between pain and suffering, change is possible."

Jon Kabat-Zinn, "At Home in Our Bodies"

6: THE DRAMA TRIANGLE

The Drama Triangle describes the unhealthy roles some of us take on in response to dramas that occur in life.[4] If we want to change the pain and unhealthy drama in our lives we might want to take a look at how we get on the drama triangle, and how to get off it.

PERSECUTOR
"TROUBLE MAKER"

Criticizes, Blames, Puts down

ATTITUDE: Sees Problems
FEELINGS: Anger, Irritation
MODE: Attack, Reactive
UNDER IT ALL: Victim

RESCUER
"SAVIOR OR FIXER"

Needs to be needed, colludes,

ATTITUDE: Problem Solver
FEELINGS: Smug, Self-Righteous
MODE: Fixit, Giving Advice
UNDER IT ALL: Victim

VICTIM
"POOR ME"

Needs to be center of attention, powerless

ATTITUDE: Complaint
FEELINGS: Anxiety, Depression, Fear
MODE: Reactive

The three positions or roles on the Drama Triangle are: Persecutor, Victim and Rescuer. When we get on the Drama Triangle, most

---

[4] "Drama Triangle" used with permission of Steven Karpman.

likely we will take on the position that we think suits us best—one we feel comfortable with and have perfected. Once on the triangle, we act out our role of choice with the people in our world— friends, family, acquaintances, etc.

When you become stuck in one of these habitual reaction styles (victim, persecutor or rescuer) this role tends to take over your life. It may even seem as if being in your particular role gives you some power. Although each role may appear to have power, in truth, they are all powerless and dependent on drama to keep them going. In order to find your true power, it would be helpful to find ways to move off the Drama Triangle.

THE PLAYERS:

THE PERSECUTOR

- Says things like "See what you did, stupid!"
- Looks for and finds victims in any situation
- Criticizes & judges others
- Adopts an angry "attack-mode"
- Often thinks they are the boss...and in control of others

Others often see the Persecutor role as the "Bad Guy," "Tough Guy" or the villain. As a Persecutor we may be the one to inspire others to jump on the Drama Triangle as either a Victim or a Rescuer.

The Persecutor is often the one who appears to instigate the Drama Triangle. But it takes more than just the Persecutor to keep the Drama Triangle rolling. The Victim position is the key point in the Triangle. It's the role around which the other two revolve.

THE VICTIM

- Takes the "Poor me" position.
- Feels helpless, hopeless, powerless, ashamed.
- Looks for a Rescuer, someone who can save or help them.
- Feels at the mercy of the Persecutor.
- Says things like "Look what you did to me." (blames everyone else).

When we are in the Victim position, we don't have to take responsibility for our actions or feelings, since everyone in the world is "doing it to me..." as in, "Hey! . . I'm the VICTIM here!!" As a Victim we look for someone or something to blame when things don't work in our life. We might blame the government, our mother, father, friends, boss, lawyer, snitches, etc. We are in the Victim position anytime we are unhappy with what is happening and blaming something or someone outside of ourselves.

A Victim is always looking for a Rescuer to take care of them, take the responsibility for, or fix whatever happened. Victims actually think they achieve control by using blame and guilt. They find someone to blame for all their woes, and then they find a Rescuer to agree with them. Who do they always blame?...The Persecutor.

Sometimes the Persecutor changes and becomes a Victim when they feel everyone is blaming them. Or they might accept the blame, feel guilty, and then try to make the situation better by attempting to become the Rescuer and fixing the situation. When the Persecutor shifts to the Rescuer or the Victim position, they avoid the guilt of being the 'Bad Guy.'

THE RESCUER

- is a fixer who says, "Let me help you!"
- Rescues others even when they don't want to be rescued.
- Feels guilty if they don't help, fix, or rescue.
- Contributes to keeping victims in the victim role.

The Rescuer is the "Good Guy." The Rescuer may choose this role out of guilt or helplessness, or a need to be effective and strong. When the Victim approaches the Rescuer with their story of woe, the Rescuer jumps on the triangle ready to "Save the Day!" As Rescuers, we believe we should take care of, or fix, other people's problems; and if we don't, we feel bad or guilty. As a Rescuer we feel obligated to help and don't want to ever look like the "Bad Guy."

Rescuers must have a Victim. They need someone to take care of, someone to control. This allows a Rescuer to feel good and powerful. Rescuers need to be needed; they need be right, no matter the cost. But in effect, because they always take care of others, they don't take care of themselves, and jeopardize their own well-being, and in turn ending up feeling like a Victim. The Rescuer then moves to blaming the situation or person they were intending to help or rescue. When the Rescuer becomes the Victim, they might say things like, "Look at all I've done for you! You owe me!"

ROLE SWITCHING

As we can see, this can become a vicious cycle, with each person jumping from role to role and flipping around the Drama Triangle endlessly. One minute we are the Victim, and the next we are the Persecutor, persecuting others who don't help us. If anyone in the Triangle changes roles, the other two roles change, as well. Generally, we don't stick to just one role; however, a lot of us have a fairly common "entry point" on to the Drama Triangle.

Which role do you most often play? After identifying which role fits you best, take some time to think about how taking on this role has either helped, or not helped, you get what you want in your life.

DRAMA HOOKS

Drama Hooks are "hot buttons" or the kind of things others say or do that "hook" you into drama; some common hooks are: blame, judgment, guilt or anger.

- THE RESCUER gets hooked by guilt.
- THE VICTIM gets hooked by feeling helpless or powerless.
- THE PERSECUTOR gets hooked by anger or feeling threatened.

These hooks fly by all day long. The key is to become really aware of what your personal 'hooks' are and then stop to choose another healthy way to respond.

HOW DO WE GET OFF THE TRIANGLE?

By now, this is a question that you might have already asked yourself.

STEPS TO GET OFF THE DRAMA TRIANGLE:

1. Recognize you are on the Drama Triangle (I'm upset, angry, afraid, breathing hard, etc.) and identify which position you are in.
2. Hold your Seat" and State Shift (State Shifting might include: taking a breath, counting to 10, taking a walk, getting some space, doing some exercise, meditating – whatever it takes to slow your reactions and shift your mind away from immediately getting on the Drama Triangle).
3. After state shifting (and when you are no longer triggered) use your voice appropriately. This can be external or internal (self-talk).

TIPS FOR USING YOUR VOICE:

- Own your feelings ("I'm angry, scared, sad, etc.").
- Use "I" (ownership) statements instead of "You" or "You are..." (blame) statements.
- State your needs clearly ("to be respected," "to have my own space," "to be included," etc.).
- Set appropriate boundaries (when necessary).

STAYING OFF THE DRAMA TRIANGLE:

- Become aware of your typical Drama Triangle roles and your personal "Drama Hooks."
- Practice mindfulness to become more aware and able to see potential dramas before they happen.

- Make clear agreements and keep them – renegotiate when necessary.
- Realize that you cannot control others – learn to let go, live and let live.
- Don't take things personally (it's not about you, what others do and say is about them).
- Don't make assumptions about others' intentions; check it out with them.
- Take responsibility for your actions so that you gain genuine personal power.

WHY WOULD WE WANT OFF?

- Being on the Drama Triangle results in:
- Chaos, craziness, sadness, grief, confusion, and anger.
- Pain & the endless loop of pain.

NO POWER
On the Triangle, we operate out of powerlessness. We go through the motions of our role like a robot or puppet being led by a puppet master.

NO CHOICE IN SIGHT
We might feel like there is no room for personal choice when we are locked into any of the roles. It is possible to flip your mind off of endless painful drama. The more you do it—the easier it gets.

MEDITATION: DIRECTOR'S CUT

Have you ever seen a movie or television show that is showing someone making a film? The director sits in their chair and yells, "Cut!" when a scene is finished. This wipes the slate so the filmmakers can finish the scene and move on.

In this meditation, you will be the Director. What you will be "cutting" is your own racing thoughts or story lines with drama. Sit down and take a few deep breaths. Let your thoughts come and go. If you notice that you are having thoughts that are creating discomfort or tension in your mind or body, silently but firmly say, "Cut!" to yourself. When you say "Cut!" you will be wiping the slate clean to experience something different. The internal voice you use when you say "cut!" should be strong and direct, but not aggressive. You are the Director of the scene that is playing in your head. You have the power to call "Cut!" and rewrite the script. Try this meditation several times this week whenever you have spinning or looping drama thoughts.

GETTING DIFFERENT RESULTS
By Dr. Amber Kelly

In one meditation class at a women's prison, a woman shared an experience she had the previous week. In past classes, she had described feeling that two officers "had it out for her." She talked about the times when they would accuse her of something, which would leave her angry and defensive. Each time she would end up in "jail" (or seg). The woman reported that last week something different happened:

"So they came up to me, and accused me of something, like always. And maybe I did do something I wasn't supposed to be doing, but they approached me in a really disrespectful way. And I started to get mad, as usual. But then I remembered that thing you told us about the breath.

So I said, in the middle of the conversation 'OK. I hear what you're saying. I just need a second to take a couple of breaths.' I think they were so shocked, they just went with it. So I put up my hand, closed my eyes, and took 2 or 3 deep breaths. As I breathed, I realized that I didn't want these guys to have control over the rest of my week. I didn't want to end up in jail. I just wanted to move on about my day. So I opened my eyes and looked at them and said 'You're right. I shouldn't have done that. I'll take responsibility.' Again, I think they were so shocked, they just sort of mouthed off to me a little more, and then went on about their business. And then I was able to go on about mine. It was crazy!

So it's not that I liked how they were speaking to me, but by stopping and breathing, I realized what my real goal was. And it changed how I responded to them. So I got different results. Wow."

"Meditation is the ultimate mobile device;
you can use it anywhere, anytime."
Sharon Salzberg, meditation teacher

8. EMPOWERMENT

THE EMPOWERMENT TRIANGLE

Every time we choose to get off the Drama Triangle, we move onto the Empowerment Triangle[5] where the Victim moves to the Creative, the Persecutor becomes the Challenger and the Rescuer becomes the Coach. The Victim is now the Creative Position, located at the top of the triangle, as a fully empowered player.

CREATIVE
CREATIVE LEARNER

ATTITUDE: Open to Possibility & New Outcomes
FEELINGS: Passion, Curiosity
MODE: Creative, Responsive & taking steps for positive results

"I CAN DO IT!"

CHALLENGER
TRUTH-TELLER

ATTITUDE: Mirror-Like Wisdom
FEELINGS: Clarity, Strength
MODE: Nudges Positive Change
"JUST DO IT!"

COACH
SUPPORTER

ATTITUDE: Encouraging, Supportive
FEELINGS: Compassion, Equanimity
MODE: Listening, Inquiry
"YOU CAN DO IT!"

---

[5] Adapted from David Emerald, "The Power of TED* (*The Empowerment Dynamic)" (Bainbridge Island, WA: Polaris Press, 2009).

THE EMPOWERED PLAYERS

THE CREATIVE

While the victim's main message to the world is "Poor poor me!", stepping into the Creative position takes you into a creative position that will allow you to look at what's possible (instead of only what's wrong) and say: "What can I do?" to change this situation. When creatively looking for different outcomes to drama, you are curious about life, patient with mistakes, and always learning and open to change. From this position you can come up with healthy, solutions to problems or challenges.

THE CHALLENGER

Unlike the Persecutor, who is always blaming or angry and self righteous, the Challenger sees clearly what's going on and isn't afraid to speak the truth. The Challenger's strength inspires change without needing to shake a finger or raise a fist. In relation to the Creative, the Challenger's message is "Just do it!"

THE COACH

Despite seemingly noble intentions, the Rescuer's "need to be needed" actually keeps the Victim in the Victim position. The Coach, however, doesn't need the Creative person to be any particular way. Instead, they listen, ask helpful questions, offer helpful suggestions and support change. The message of the Coach is "You can do it!"

AN EMPOWERING VIEW

With Empowerment, we choose our position, and the way we see others. Example: Persecutors are Challengers in disguise, "inspiring" us to practice (e.g., by holding our seat). Rescuers can be seen as

supporters, etc. We can simply see the behavior of others as a chance to challenge ourselves to grow.

WHAT IS POWER?

Who do you think is in charge of your life?
Who has power over you?
Do you ever feel powerless?
Do you ever look for ways to get power over others?
Do you lash out when you think people have power or control over you?

This session is about empowerment, which is a term used to describe healthy power. Power is not simply about controlling others, it's a strong energy that can be used to create healthy lives and communities. In this session, we will look at ways that power can benefit us, rather than lead us down a path of trouble

Choosing to step out of the Victim role and into the Creative role is a giant leap on the Path of Freedom. When we make that leap we gain a lot of power in our lives. But what exactly does that power look like?

Most people think that power means strength or control. What do you think power means? Is it about being decisive, strong, muscular, successful, a "winner?" How about forceful, tyrannical, controlling, or dominating? Is power found in the barrel of a gun?

All of these qualities represent the unhealthy side of power. Power can be used to destroy, as well as to create positive change. Power can be used to harm or to help people. The unhealthy side of power fuels the drama triangle and creates trouble in our lives.

If we keep our definition of power to an idea like Power = Control, we will never be able to let go of control for fear of losing power. Sticking with a definition of power like that can trap us in fear or anxiety. Then we are trapped in continually worrying about being controlled or controlling others.

"We can let the circumstances of life harden us so we become resentful and afraid, or we can let them soften us and make us kinder. We always have the choice."
H.H. Dalai Lama,
Nobel Prize Winner

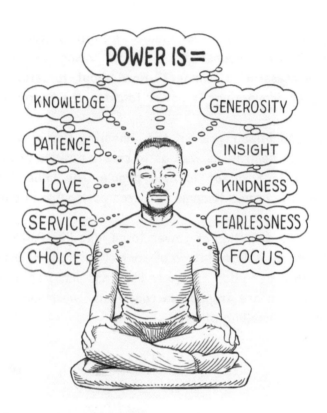

THE GOOD IN POWER

Another way to think about power is to look at the empowered, good side of it. Being empowered also means knowing where we can use power in its unhealthy forms and choosing not to as well as choosing to focus on the power we can use for the good.

Power comes from the body, the mind, and the emotions. How we work with, and realize our own healthy power, is a path or a journey. The Path of Freedom teaches the art of being an empowered, compassionate person and how to have power with others rather than power over others.

THE POWER OF CHOICE
The Twelve Choices of An Empowered Person

1. **VALUES BEING HUMAN**—choosing to see worth and goodness in ourselves and others, rather than the brokenness.
2. **APPRECIATION**–the choice to appreciate that life is precious.
3. **MINDFULNESS + AWARENESS**-the choice to be present and awake.
4. **UNHOOK FROM DRAMA**-the choice to boycott drama.
5. **OWNERSHIP + RESPONSIBILITY**-the choice to be responsible for our own thoughts, feelings, and actions.
6. **INTEGRITY**-the choice be decent, honest, truthful, and kind.
7. **REFRAMING**-the choice to see problems as challenges and opportunities–rather than defeat and despair.
8. **LIVING POSSIBILITY**-the choice to see possibility rather than only seeing obstacles.
9. **SPEAKING PEACE**-the choice to listen carefully and speak gently.
10. **FORGIVENESS**-the choice to forgive ourselves and others, to let go and move on.
11. **GENEROSITY**-the choice to share and give without expecting anything in return.

12. GRATITUDE–the choice to be satisfied with what we have, instead of obsessing on what we don't have or what we think we should have.

TAKE BACK THE POWER

We've all seen our favorite basketball star taking a shot from the free throw line. He stands there in front of thousands of screaming fans and makes a shot while fans from the other team scream and yell, trying to distract him from making the shot. If the player is not focused on the basket, and allows the chaos around him to distract him, he's probably not going to make it in the NBA. This kind of focus is what makes a star. Without focus, the mind becomes distracted and the shot is missed.

Do you let the screaming fans of your thoughts distract you? Without focus, we will be powerless to every thought that pops up. When a thought comes up, do you react to it without even thinking about it? If someone makes you angry, what is your first reaction? To strike out? Maybe punch somebody or yell at them and call them names? Just like in basketball, this is how we miss our moment of choice and power. This is how the shot gets missed; the basket is missed altogether. We do have a choice in how we react. Our minds can be unfocused and distracted, but we have the ability to train the mind to have the focus of an NBA star. We do this through mindfulness practice.

When you are walking around, going to lunch or in the exercise yard, notice what really pisses you off. When someone is really loud and brags about how tough they are, does that annoy you? It might get to you, but if you get pissed, and start yelling, you've given them the power. If in your head you accuse them of making you act out and distracting you from your focus or goal, you've given them the power. Sometimes the only real power you have is the power to control your own reactions.

Easier said than done. When you are pissed and feel the rage build up inside you, your body tenses and your heart starts to beat faster, and all you want is to DO SOMETHING! You might want to hit or yell at someone or something. You might think someone is doing something to you. But in fact, no one is in control of you and your reactions, but you. Stop! Take a deep breath. Take several deep breaths. Train your mind to focus sharply on your breath and not on your mental reaction.

By doing this you are taking back your power. You are owning the power that you have, rather than giving it to someone else by getting lost in your reaction. This short breather is what allows you to keep up your focus and sink the shot, despite the drama that sometimes steals your attention. Once you get good at this, once you no longer react so quickly to the distractions of your mind, you are in control, you have the power. The cool thing about using your breath to calm down is that it also helps with the other things that are going on with you as well. Things like depression, negativity, or hopelessness. You might be caught up in stories about how powerless you are. True, you may not be able to change the situation that you are in, and in a lot of ways you might feel powerless, but find the place where you do have the power and claim it. You have the power of focusing your mind to achieve peace and calm. You have the power to stop chain reactions. Try it!

"When the power of love overcomes the love of power, the world will know peace."
~Jimi Hendrix, Musician.

NOBLE SILENCE

Do you talk a lot? If you do, you might talk about worries, opinions, ideas, complaints, things that have happened, experiences, what you want, and so on. Maybe you spend time talking about others—gossiping and judging them. Maybe you go through life riding on a speedy thought train and talking quickly about whatever pops in your head. Have you ever gotten so worn out from talking that you just needed some silence and peace?

Noble Silence is not about forcing ourselves to be quiet. Noble Silence is the experience of peace inside, of carrying ourselves with honor, respect and an inner quiet. In holding ourselves this way, we build an inner peace and strength inside, holding ourselves as regally as a Queen or King. As inner silence becomes part of our lives, we begin to notice that impulses that used to rule us are ruling us less. We start to slow down and find more things to enjoy. As you begin this practice, you might even enjoy silence itself and find it nourishing. You might find you stop anxiously filling up silence with talk or noise.

Noble Silence is an attitude, or a shift, in how you view yourself in the world. It is also a posture of openness, curiosity, and anticipation.

It's like being at a movie theater when the lights dim, and the film is about to start. Everyone waits, quiet and still. Noble Silence is the precious gap before the drama begins again.

NOBLE SILENCE MEDITATION

Shut your eyes. Take a deep, full breath. Take your seat comfortably with your back straight, dignified but relaxed and regal like a King or Queen. Close your eyes and just breathe. Now is the time for you to experience Noble Silence.

Thoughts will happen, just allow them to pass like clouds drifting across the sky. Notice any sensations, feelings or thoughts that appear. Simply notice them.

Find a still, quiet, silent place inside yourself. Imagine yourself melting into the deep quiet stillness.

Then bring your attention to your heart area. Breathe deeply into it, expanding the chest, and belly. Let your exhale fall softly. Imagine a warmth in your heart area as if you heart was like the sun. Feel the warmth and light. Now, open your eyes and look around and imagine sending this warmth and light out to the world. Like the sun, you don't need to do or be anything other than who you are. Simply rest in the strength of your own basic warmth, and let it spread out beyond you. Stay with this feeling for a few minutes.

"The most common way people give up their power
is by thinking they don't have any."

Alice Walker, Writer

9. THE ART OF COMMUNICATION

"When we understand the needs that motivate our own and others' behavior, we have no enemies."
Marshall Rosenberg, Author

Learning to communicate with skill is an art that can change your life. How many problems have you had because of things that were said (or unsaid)?

LISTENING

Skillful communication begins with listening - we all like to be heard. Listening to another person shows respect. We all probably know what it's like to express something and feel that no one is listening to us. Some people even think that the opposite of talking is not listening . . . it's waiting for the other to just stop talking so that they can talk. Listening involves hearing another human being in a deeply respectful way. Learning to listen in ways that others know they are heard is a skill that will serve you all your days.

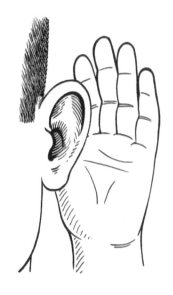

"Empathic Listening" is feeling what's going on with someone else, and asking yourself the question: "What's it like to be them?"

STYLES OF LISTENING

COCOON LISTENING:

In this style, we sort of notice someone is out there speaking, but our motive for listening is habit and fear. We are lost in our own world of self-defense. We hear others speak, but it's like a faint echo in the distance. We are so focused on ourselves that we ignore others. This style could also be called "Not Listening."

DAYDREAMING AT THE EDGE OF COCOON:

We know someone is talking to us, but we are listening to see if their words line up with our version of reality. It's as if we are saying to ourselves "yes," "no." "yes" "no." "I "agree." "I disagree." Back and forth. We might sometimes nod or agree (or "mmhmm""... or even say "yes") when something they say fits with our own ideas, but we are basically just waiting for them to finish so we can give our own views. This is a type of listening that grown-ups do with children. This style disregards others' views. We try to place our own ideas on whatever anyone expresses. People often respond to this type of listening by saying "You're not listening!" or "Would you please listen?!"

STEPPING OUT OF COCOON:

Here, we are now really with someone else and see that they have thoughts separate from our own. But still, we are understanding their feelings for largely selfish reasons or even as a fact-gathering mission to build a case. This style of listening is attentive to the words of others but is focused on data only. We are not noticing any nonverbal signals or their body language in general. This style is fine for fact-gathering, but not great for communication in relationships. 'Data only' listening can be manipulative. It "wins battles and loses wars."

LISTENING:

Here, we are now relating to another human being. This style is sometimes called 'active listening.' Our own thoughts come up, but they are like clouds in an open sky; we might notice them, but we allow them to float by while we listen. We listen to the person's words, the tone of their voice, and even notice their body language. We take note of facial expressions. Even with all this, this style is still 'one way' communication, empty of emotion on our part. We are still on the fact-gathering level. Active listening is sometimes practiced by therapists and can have a manipulative or 'Rescuer' edge to it.

EMPATHIC LISTENING:

Here, we are relating and feeling (not overly identifying with their feelings and needs though). We feel their story and seek to understand and connect to what they need. We ask clarifying questions to help someone to find their own wisdom. We are able to clearly mirror back what they are trying to tell us. We listen with full attention to the sounds and other signals, including: tone of voice, pace of voice, body language, feelings, and needs.

"When someone really hears you without passing judgment on you, without trying to take responsibility for you, without trying to mold you, it feels damn good."

Carl Rogers, Psychotherapist

GIVING EMPATHY

Empathy is the ability to understand and feel the emotions of others. We learn empathy through receiving it from others. It is difficult to feel it for others if we have not experienced it ourselves. The first step in learning how to give empathy is to give it to ourselves.

Responding with empathy allows us to truly 'not take it personally.' It moves us beyond criticism and blame, allowing us to see under the stories and behaviors and into what's really happening. As we develop the skill, we begin to see that all unpleasant behavior stems from unmet needs. As we begin to understand these needs, we see how similar they are to our own.

Being empathic does not mean that we necessarily agree with behavior that we think is wrong. It simply means understanding where someone is coming from and having some compassion for the fact that all of us sometimes make the wrong (unskillful) choices to meet our needs. Try this: the next time you see someone doing something you don't like, stop and reflect for a moment on what that person might need. Listen, not to their stories, words, or behaviors but simply listen to the need that is alive in that moment. You might be surprised or even touched if you really 'hear' what they need.

"I've seen it many times, the point when a person in prison really 'gets' empathy and connects with the suffering of others in a compassionate way, this is the point when their life turns around for the better."
Fleet Maull, Author and former prisoner

HABITUAL RESPONSES

Below are more of the habitual ways of responding that are not empathic. Do you recognize any in yourself or in others? Can you see how these aren't quite helpful?

GIVING ADVICE/FIXING:
Telling the other person what you think they should do: "You should leave your wife and find somebody better to be with."

ANALYZING/DIAGNOSING:
Evaluating a person's behavior: "You are taking this out on your friend when, in reality, you are angry with your mother about things that happened in your childhood."

SHIFTING FOCUS TO ME:
Moving the focus and story away from the other and back to yourself: "I know just how you feel! This reminds me of a time that I..."

SYMPATHY:
This type of response is more about your feelings than theirs: "I feel really bad for you."

POLLYANNA:
Trying to make the person 'feel better' by telling them things will improve: "Tomorrow's another day!" "You might be upset now, but I'm sure you will feel better soon."

SHUTTING DOWN/DISCOUNTING:
"Forget about it!" "It's no big deal!" "Who cares?" "Stop feeling sorry for yourself!" or, "Knock it off!"

CORRECTING/CRITICIZING:
Giving the person your opinion about a situation: "Wait a minute – I never said that!" or, "You're full of it!"

INTERROGATING/FACT FINDING:
Using directed questions to 'expose' or try to change their behavior: "When did this begin?" or, "Why did you do that?" or, "What got into you?"

COLLUDING:
Enjoying the blame game and agreeing with the speaker's judgment of others: "I know what you mean – that guy is one of the biggest jerks I have ever met!"

ONE-UPPING:
Convincing the speaker that whatever they went through, you had it worse: "You think that's bad? Let me tell you what happened to ME when I was in that situation!"

AVOIDING:
"mmm....humm" "yeah..." Detached – in other words, not listening.

ENTERTAINMENT/HOOKED ON STORY:
Getting caught up in the 'entertainment' value of the story. Encouraging them to do more complaining or storytelling.

UNMET NEEDS DRIVE BEHAVIOR AND WORDS

Have you noticed that sometimes the way you talk doesn't help you get what you want? Do others ever get defensive or respond like they didn't hear what you said? Marshall Rosenberg created a model for communication called "Nonviolent Communication" (NVC). He said, "Everything anyone does (or says) is an attempt to meet a basic human need and to make their life more wonderful."

Stop and think about this for a moment—think of someone that does something that you label 'bad.' Have there been times when someone has labeled something you've done 'bad'? How did that feel? Was it true? Consider that everything people do is an attempt to meet a need. Needs are not bad nor good, they are simply part of the richness of life. With empathy, we throw out labels of 'Good' and 'Bad' and try to understand the unmet need under what people are saying or doing.

For example, when we have a need for respect, and it's not being met, and then we yell at someone and say, "GIVE ME SOME RESPECT!" We probably won't get the respect we hoped for. Demanding from others that they meet our needs rarely works.

GIVE ME RESPECT!!

Sometimes we get so caught up in our emotions that we act quickly, without being clear about what we need. NVC suggests taking a moment to really connect with what we feel and need. Then, after getting clear about what we need (example: needing respect), we can figure out ways to communicate first, with ourself, and then with others, so that we might get our needs met.

THE FOUR COMPONENTS OF NONVIOLENT COMMUNICATION (NVC)

as taught by Marshall Rosenberg, Ph.D[6]

- Observations
- Identifying your Feelings
- Identifying your Needs
- Requesting what will meet your Needs

STEP ONE: OBSERVATIONS

How do you describe what is going on with you? Do you use labels, judgments, or criticism? Practicing NVC, we learn to make clear observations.

"**Observation without evaluation is the highest form of human intelligence.**"

J. Krishnamurti, Philosopher

EXAMPLE:
Judgment: "You always talk on the phone for too long."
Observation "I stood in line behind you for 30 minutes while you talked on the phone."

Words like "always," "never," etc. are vague and judgmental. "Too long" is also a judgment, what is "too long" for me, may not be "too long" for you. So, why would you want to express yourself without judgment? Because by clearly and honestly expressing ourselves, others often respond with less defensiveness and more openness.

---

[6] Marshall B. Rosenberg, Nonviolent Communication: The Language of Life. (Puddle Dancer Press, Encinitas, CA)

You may have noticed that defensiveness tends to quickly lead conversations downhill into conflict. Most people don't enjoy being told what to think about things. They like to form their own opinions. So clean observations simply state the facts.

Using NVC, you get rid of types of communication that block compassion. Certain ways of speaking remove us from our natural state of basic goodness. Examples: judgments ("He's lazy!"), labels, comparisons, denial of responsibility ("I did it 'cause I just had to!"), and demands ("you should" or, "you must ...").

STEP 1: OBSERVATION PRACTICE

QUESTIONS: Which of these statements express observations, free of judgments or assumptions:

1. "He looked pissed off."
2. "She was talking louder than I enjoy."
3. "His forehead began to wrinkle up."
4. "Her voice sounded angry."
5. "He's a slob! He always leaves dishes in the sink!"
6. "He told me that he wanted me to turn off the light three times."
7. "He definitely wanted to fight me."

ANSWERS:

1. Not an observation. The speaker is assuming the other person's emotional state from a facial expression.
2. Observation. Simply expresses the speaker's feelings.
3. Observation. Describes what the speaker saw.
4. Not observation. Speaker assumes what the other person is feeling. You can't be sure what someone feels unless they tell you.
5. Not Observation. Speaker is evaluating ("slob" and "always").
6. Observation. Speaker is observing what actually happened without drawing conclusions.
7. Not observation. Speaker is assuming what the other person wanted to do based on his/her perceptions.

STEP 2: IDENTIFYING FEELINGS

Why do some of us push our feelings away? We do this for different reasons. Being real with our emotions takes a lot of courage. Some of us grew up in families where people just didn't show emotion. Some of us might have stopped trusting other people because of things that have happened to us in the past. We might decide there are only two things to do with feelings: stuff them down or act them out. When we stuff feelings down, over and over, they build up and can become destructive to our lives and relationships. When we impulsively act out our feelings, we can end up in trouble and with more problems.

Feelings are an important part of life, they are signals or messages, that our needs may or may not be getting met. It's an important skill to be able to identify and be clear about what we feel and especially what we need. Learning how to sit with our feelings and hear the message they are sending us about unmet needs is a life changing and powerful practice.

"IMPOSTER" FEELINGS

These are words that people use to describe feelings that are actually thoughts or judgments. They might be true and accurate judgments, but they aren't true feelings.

abandoned	abused	betrayed
distrusted	ignored	intimidated
interrupted	let down	manipulated
misunderstood	neglected	pressured
provoked	put down	rejected
talked down to	unseen	unheard
unsupported	unwanted	used

FEELINGS EXERCISE:

PART ONE: MET NEEDS: Think of a situation where you felt great and things were going your way. Read the words below and circle those that you felt. (Feelings that might come up when your needs are being met).

Affection	Alert	Alive
Amused	Animated	Appreciative
Amazed	Awake	Blissful
Calm	Centered	Cheerful
Chill	Clear	Comfortable
Confident	Contented	Curious
Delighted	Eager	Empowered
Energetic	Enthusiastic	Excited
Engaged	Exhilarated	Ecstatic
Elated	Friendly	Free
Glad	Grateful	Happy
Healthy	Interested	Invigorated
Inspired	Involved	Intrigued
Joy	Loving	Lively
Mellow	Mindful	Moved
Open	Optimistic	Passionate
Peaceful	Proud	Relaxed
Respected	Rested	Restored
Revived	Relaxed	Safe
Satisfied	Secure	Steady
Stimulated	Tender	Thankful
Thrilled	Touched	Trusting
Valued	Vital	Warm
Wonder	Zest	

PART TWO: UNMET NEEDS: Think of a time, or conflict, when things didn't go your way. Circle the words below that describe how you felt. (Feelings when needs are not met).

Aloof	Anguish	Angry
Annoyed	Aggravated	Alienated
Anxious	Ashamed	Aversion
Alarmed	Anxiety	Beat
Burnt out	Bored/Cold	Bitter
Contempt	Confused	Dismay
Disappointed	Depressed	Disheartened
Despair	Dissatisfied	Discouraged
Distress	Dazed	Disconnected
Disgust	Distant	Deflated
Dislike	Dread	Distracted
Embarrassed	Exasperated	Envy
Edgy	Fatigue	Furious
Frustrated	Frazzled	Fear
Gloomy	Guilty	Grief
Heartbroken	Hurt	Hate
Heavy	Hopeless	Hesitant
Helpless	Hostile	Impatient
Irritated	Irate	Indignant
Irritable	Indifferent	Jealous
Longing	Lonely	Lost
Leery	Miffed	Miserable
Nervous	Numb	Outraged
Overwhelm	Pessimistic	Pissed
Pain	Passive	Pining
Panicked	Puzzled	Resentful
Resentment	Regretful	Restless
Sad	Self-conscious	Shocked
Startled	Sluggish	Surprised
Suspicious	Stressed	Troubled
Tense	Tired	Unhappy
Unclear	Uncertain	Upset
Wretched	Withdrawn	Worried

STEP 3: RECOGNIZING NEEDS

NEEDS EXERCISE:

Use the same conflict on the previous page where you identified the feelings present. Now circle all the needs listed below that were not met in the situation.

Acceptance
Awareness
Appreciation
Choice
Creativity
Community
Consistency
Competenc
Empathy
Fresh Air
Freedom
Growth
Harmony
Intimacy
Inclusion/Belonging
Loyalty
Love
Order
Peace
Reassurance
Space
Self Worth
Seen (for who you are)
Shelter
Understanding

Autonomy
Authenticity (being true to yourself)
Balance
Closeness
Connection
Consideration
Companionship
Dependability
Effectiveness
Family
Fun & Play
Health
Honesty
Independence
Integrity
Laughter
Mourning Loss
Protection
Participation
Relaxation
Spontaneity
Self Respect
Self ExpressioN
Sleep
Warmth

Adventure
Beauty
Challenge
Celebration
Cooperation
Clarity
Exercise
Equality
Friendship
Food
Humor
Hope
Inspiration
Knowledge
Learning
Meaning
Purpose
Respect
Safety
Spirituality
Support
Security
Trust
Wisdom

STEP 4: REQUESTS

So, how do we get our needs met? The first step might be to look at what we can do to meet our own needs rather than demanding that others meet them. As in the previous example, maybe we want to be respected. What can we do if there seems to be no one to give us the respect we need? We can find a way to connect with the care and respect inside ourselves.

For example, reading this book, might be a way to meet your need for respect on some level. Here you are respecting yourself enough to find ways to grow, learn, and work with your pain. The exercise you just did is another way to respect yourself, since you are taking the time to really check in with what is going on for you. Look around and begin to notice all the ways respect shows up in your life.

Yet, even when we do include these new ways of getting our needs met, we sometimes would like to have some help or support from the outside. That's where the skill of "requesting what you need" comes in.

Have you ever blamed someone when they didn't meet your needs? For most of us, that doesn't usually work out well. Demanding people meet our needs doesn't work either. How do you feel when you are told what you "should" do? Do you respond well to being bossed? Probably not. Clean requests come from a place of possibility, not ultimatum. We invite someone to join with us, instead of demanding they do what we want them to.

When we make a request, the other person has every right to say "No." It's possible that this just isn't the right time for them to help us. If we get a "No" after we make a request, and we freak out, that's shows that we made a demand, not a request. When we think someone is demanding something of us, we tend to feel pressured, and will try to get the pressure off our backs.

At this point try opening yourself to other possibilities—there are billions of people on the planet, maybe we can find someone else to help us? When we get really stuck on the 'fact' that only this one person could meet our needs, well, there might be something wrong with this picture.

Requests should be as specific, detailed, clear, and as positive as possible. Detail leaves less room for misinterpretation. Positive language works better also, because not many of us like to hear "don't do . . . this or that." A helpful way to begin a request is, "Would you be willing to . . .?"

QUESTION:
Which of these statements are requests and not demands:

1. "Would you please leave the room right now?"
2. "I want you to stop talking to me like I'm an idiot."
3. "Treat me with respect!"
4. "Would you be willing to not tell anyone about the stuff I told you about myself last night?"
5. "Would you be willing to stop bothering me?"
6. "Would you be willing to tell me when you think I am not listening to you?"
7. "I want you to stop being so pissed."

ANSWERS:

1. Request: speaker asks for a specific action.
2. Demand: speaker isn't clear about what the other person said, and what they want specifically done.
3. Demand: speaker isn't saying what specifically constitutes respect.
4. Request: speaker made a specific request.

5. Too Vague a Request: speaker doesn't tell the other person specific actions that would keep another from bothering him/her.
6. Request: speaker is asking for specific actions.
7. Too Vague a Request: speaker doesn't tell the other what actions can be taken to meet the speaker's need.

"Say what you mean, mean what you say, don't say it mean."
Participant, POF Prison Class

SELF-EMPATHY

This involves clearly naming and understanding our own feelings and needs in any situation. After we are clear about what's going on with us, we can reflect on our feelings and needs. What we tend to do when we need something is race ahead to a usual strategy without being clear if it's the best way in that moment. Self-Empathy practice helps slow down the process so that we can be clear about our choices (the exercises we just did in this chapter was a form of Self-Empathy practice). Once we master the ability to give ourselves empathy, we have an easier time empathizing with others. Empathy is about understanding the struggle we all sometimes have when trying to get our needs met.

By being empathic (instead of giving advice, making fun, or criticizing), communication becomes more positive and effective. Most people tend to respond to empathy feeling thankful that they are being heard. How do you feel when someone really listens to you and understands what is going on with you?

LISTENING MEDITATION

In this meditation, you will focus on everything that you hear, using sound as the focus of your meditation. Sounds, just like thoughts, come and go and are impermanent.

INSTRUCTIONS:

Be very still and quiet. Stillness allows our hearing to be more sensitive. Most of the time we don't hear what is going on around us because we are so distracted by our own thoughts and internal noise.

After you settle and are still, just listen. Wait and listen for sounds to arise. No need to look for the sounds, they will show up.

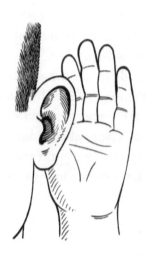

When you begin to notice the sounds, you might find that you are silently naming where the sounds are coming from ('door shutting' or 'voices talking' or 'feet moving' etc.). Sometimes you might judge the sounds as being '"too loud" or "annoying." Or you might be attracted to the sounds and want to just hear them.

Simply sit still and listen. Focus on the tone or quality of the sounds you hear, rather than where sounds are coming from. After a while, your thoughts about the sounds will slow down, and you will simply hear the sounds without having to name them.

Just be with the sounds...just listen. Try this for five minutes.

"METTA" MEDITATION

Metta is a word that means "loving-kindness." When you are experiencing pain, isn't it helpful to have someone around who cares about you and who is kind? Learning how to practice Metta allows us to become that kind of person for ourselves.

In this practice, we repeat certain phrases over and over. Don't expect to feel waves of wonderful emotions immediately when you do this practice, although you might. Whatever you feel, or whatever this practice brings up, is okay. Its power is in focusing on possibility. It is not about forcing feelings to happen.

If you find your mind wandering, just bring it back to the words without judgment or harshness. If you have to begin again, over and over again, that's fine. Letting go of distractions and being able to return to the practice is a basic skill of meditation.

METTA INSTRUCTIONS

Sit comfortably with your spine straight. Close your eyes. If you are sleepy, practice with your eyes open.

The four statements are:
"May I be safe."
"May I be happy."
"May I be healthy."
"May I be peaceful."

Repeat these over and over in your mind, slowly. Repeat them at a steady pace. If your mind wanders, don't worry. That's what minds do. Simply return to repeating the statements. Try this for three to five minutes.

CONTEMPLATION:
Sit for a while and think about this phrase: "Anything a person does is an attempt to make their life more wonderful." As you go through your week, see if you can notice what people are feeling and needing (perhaps on TV, the dining room, etc).

INSTRUCTIONS FOR CONTEMPLATION:
Meditate for a few minutes to stabilize your mind.
Then bring to mind the phrase or word you are contemplating.
Repeat this word or phrase (silently) over and over.
Notice and be present to what arises: images, memories, associations, and feelings. Stay present. As you begin to really experience the quality, or meaning of the word or phrase you are contemplating, simply rest in that quality, meaning, or feeling.

9. TRANSFORMING CONFLICT

"If you want to make peace, you don't talk to your friends. Talk to your enemies."
Mother Teresa, Catholic nun

Conflicts happen because our beliefs, values, and desires are not always the same as everyone else's. Conflict is a natural part of life. It can be healthy for growth and change. When poorly managed, however, it can be destructive.

Mindfulness is a powerful tool in any conflict. The more we are able to hold our seat and stay in our Adult mindset, the more access we will have to our own natural smarts, creativity, healthy personal power, and the ability to bounce back.

"Education is the ability to listen to almost anything without losing your temper or your self-confidence."
Robert Frost, Poet

MINDFULNESS PRACTICES FOR CONFLICT:

BEING MINDFUL OF YOUR BODY
Helps you to notice what happens in your body, and how it responds to conflict (adrenaline rush, muscle tightness, changes in breathing, etc.).

BEING MINDFUL OF YOUR TONE OF VOICE
Will allow you to recognize if you are "triggered" or reactive. Once you notice this, you can then lower your voice and express yourself calmly and confidently.

BEING MINDFUL OF YOUR BODY LANGUAGE
Will increase your ability to relax any defensive, tight, or aggressive postures (leaning in, clenched fists, tight jaw, scowling, etc.). Body language sends powerful messages to others that may alert the fight, fight or freeze parts of the brain. Relax your body. Uncross your arms.

BEING MINDFUL OF YOUR BREATH
Notice if it's fast, slow, shallow, or deep. Being mindful of your breathing encourages you to take deep belly breaths and remember: "The breath is your ally!"

BEING MINDFUL OF FEELING YOUR FEET
Is a great tool that will quickly take you out of your head (and storyline) and connect you with the earth under your feet, helping you to feel more present and 'grounded.' Feeling your feet also helps with looping thoughts.

BEING MINDFUL OF YOUR THOUGHTS
Allows you to notice any racing thoughts and label them "thinking." You can add calming self-talk such as, "This will pass!" or, "I'm Okay." Or you can use the 'Director's Cut' technique to snap you more into the present moment with clarity.

BEING MINDFUL OF YOUR WORDS

Helps you stay silent when triggered. It will also help you remember to use "I" statements to show ownership of your words rather than "You" statements that show blame and make others defensive.

"Why are you upset? You're believing what you think. Want to get sane? Question what you believe."
Byron Katie, Spiritual Teacher

50/50 OR 100%?

Remember this—relationship is not 50/50. What we put on the table is 100% our responsibility and what others contribute is 100% their responsibility. All we can do is be responsible and accountable for our own 100%. We are responsible for "our side of the street." We have no control over what others do. No one can make us feel or behave in any particular way. How we handle any situation is our choice. We are responsible for the outcome.

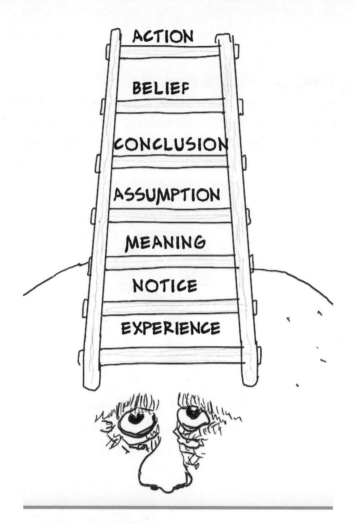

CLIMBING THE LADDER

"Climbing the Ladder" is a process developed by Chris Argyris[7]. In this model, the "Ladder of Inference" demonstrates how the mind works in conflict. It shows us how quickly we form beliefs, assumptions, and behaviors. The important thing to remember is that we can choose to climb the ladder or not. With mindfulness, we can stop at any step to consider our options, and decide whether to go up, down, or stay where we are.

---

[7]The "Ladder of Inference" was originally articulated by Chris Argyris and popularized in Peter Senge's book The Fifth Discipline: The Art and Practice of the Learning Organization (New York: Doubleday, 1990).

1ST STEP: THE EXPERIENCE

The first step on the ladder is The Experience. These are the plain facts—like what a video would show if the situation were filmed. If the video were played back, everyone would agree with what had happened.

2ND STEP: WHAT I NOTICE

We can't see everything that happens in a situation, so we choose to pay attention to certain things. We tend to notice what we think are the most important details. Different people will notice different things based on their past experiences and beliefs. This is an important step. What we notice can seriously affect our decisions. If our mind is clear and calm, we can notice things more accurately.

3RD STEP: I ADD MEANING

The third rung is called I Add Meaning, where we make what we notice personal. For example, let's say someone hit his head by accident, and you happen to come around the corner right after it happened. The person is in pain because he just hurt himself. He's not mad at you, and might not even know you, but he's looking at you with a contorted and possibly angry expression. You don't know that he just hit his head, so you begin to wonder why he is looking at you that way. You start thinking he's pissed off for some reason. Here you begin to add meaning to what we notice.

4TH STEP: I MAKE ASSUMPTIONS

Maybe the meaning you added is that he's pissed off. Then, because he happens to be looking in your direction, you assume he is angry with you. This idea is based on what you noticed (a contorted expression on his face) and the meaning you give (he's pissed off). You can see how things might get really out of hand once we climb to the Assumption step.

5TH STEP: I DRAW CONCLUSIONS

This stage is when you might officially decide that this guy is angry at you, that it's personal, and you are in danger. Although this might seem logical, it's not based on what's actually happening.

6TH STEP: I FORM BELIEFS

This is when you begin to believe that this guy doesn't like you and he's a dangerous, aggressive person who you must avoid at all costs. You might even decide to take a tough posture, challenge the person, or strike out, first in imagined self-defense. You might develop a negative internal story that no one on the planet likes you, or that something is basically wrong with you since people get mad at you for no reason. You might flashback to another time when this sort of thing happened. You then use all this to justify your belief that people are dangerous jerks, or that no one likes you, or that something is really wrong with you.

It's important to remember that this is only going on in your mind. You are almost to the top of the ladder. The other person is just standing there, maybe thinking, "Damn, I'm such a freaking idiot for banging my head." He might see you and be embarrassed because he was so clumsy. Who knows what that person was thinking, the main thing is that you weren't even on his mind.

FINAL STEP: I DO (OR DON'T) TAKE ACTION

This is where you can get yourself into trouble. In our example, you might decide to just ignore the person, mind your own business, and go on your way. In that case, you decided not to take action and everything's cool. But you might also decide to get in the person's face for scowling in your direction. Now you've got a situation on your hands. The outcome won't be pleasant or peaceful – and, most importantly, it could have easily been avoided.

The best way to slow your climb up the ladder is through nonaggressive communication. What would happen if, when you noticed the person looking at you all pissed off, you simply asked, "Hey, what's up with you?" That gives him the opportunity to say "I just banged my head, that's what. It hurts like hell, too." End of story and you climb back down the first step of the ladder.

THE EMPTY BOAT (A ZEN STORY)[8]

A man is enjoying himself on a river at dusk. He sees another boat coming down the river toward him. At first he thinks it's so nice that someone else is enjoying the river on a pleasant summer evening. Then he realizes that the boat is coming right toward him, faster and faster. He begins to get upset and starts to yell, "Hey! Hey! Watch out! For Pete's sake, turn aside!" But the boat just comes faster and faster, right toward him. By this time he's standing up in his boat, screaming and shaking his fist, and then the boat smashes right into him.

Shaking, upset and still yelling and cursing the occupant of the other boat, he suddenly sees that the other boat is empty, no one to blame or be upset with. (Moral of the story: things are not always as they seem).

---

8 Pema Chodron, Start Where You Are (Boston, MA: Shambhala Publications, 1994).

THE FOUR AGREEMENTS OF DON MIGUEL RUIZ

The author Don Miguel Ruiz. talks about Four Agreements[9] from the Toltec (Aztec spirituality) tradition. These Four Agreements are:

1. BE IMPECCABLE WITH YOUR WORD

2. DON'T TAKE ANYTHING PERSONALLY

3. DON'T MAKE ASSUMPTIONS

4. DO YOUR BEST

These are agreements you could make with yourself and use as 'slogans' or contemplations in your daily life. All four are helpful, but the middle two are especially helpful during conflict. "Don't take anything personally" is about realizing that the things others say and do are not because of you, but a reflection of their own life story and mind state. Although your words and actions might stimulate a reaction, it's still helpful to 'not take it personally'. The more you make yourself immune to others' opinions and actions, the less you will suffer. If you take this one agreement to heart, it could change your entire life.

"Don't make assumptions" was discussed earlier in the "Climbing the Ladder" material. This agreement is about getting the facts about what's really happening before leaping into your personal story. It involves developing communication skills such as asking what is happening with someone else before making up a story or making an assumption. If you find yourself "climbing the ladder" and acting from an assumption, conclusion, or belief, stop and ask yourself, "Is that really true?" Repeatedly asking that question will take you back to the underlying assumptions and allow you to check them out, bringing you back down the ladder in the process. This slogan can be transformative if you use it daily.

---

[9] Don Miguel Ruiz The Four Agreements: A Practical Guide to Personal Freedom A Toltec Wisdom Book (San Rafael, CA: Amber-Allen Publishing, 1997)

"If we could read the secret history of our enemies... we should find in each man's life sorrow and suffering enough to disarm all hostility."
Henry Wadsworth Longfellow, poet

COMPASSION MEDITATION

Shut your eyes and think about someone you really, really don't like and don't get along with — someone you have no feelings of warmth or kindness toward whatsoever. See this person in your minds eye. Read the statements below slowly, giving each one time to sink in. After each line, close your eyes and spend a few moments contemplating it as you think about the person. Take five deep breaths in between each statement.

With all your attention on this person . . . say silently to yourself: "Just like me, this person wants to be happy."

With all your attention on this person . . . say silently to yourself: "Just like me, this person does not want to feel pain."

With all your attention on this person . . . say silently to yourself: "Just like me, this person wants to be free from worries and stress."

With all your attention on this person . . . say silently to yourself: "Just like me, this person has felt sad, lonely, or hopeless at times."

With all your attention on this person . . . say silently to yourself: "Just like me, this person wants to be treated with respect."

With all your attention on this person . . . say silently to yourself: "Just like me, this person is trying to get their needs met."

Afterwards, notice any shifts in your thinking about this person. Were there times when you were stuck and unable to visualize? Why? Do this meditation daily for one week. See if you experience any changes in the way you think or feel about the person.

CONTEMPLATION: "I'M TELLING MYSELF"[10]

Think of an assumption or belief you have—something you accept and believe as absolutely true. Something you take for granted and never question.

Now ask yourself: "How do I know it's really true? Is there any possibility it is something I'm just telling myself?" For example, if you think someone doesn't like you (and they haven't told you this directly), are you certain it's true? How do you know? By their words? Body language? Actions? Are you certain that what they really feel about you?

Form your assumption or belief into a sentence such as "I believe people are out to get me." Or "I assume so-and-so is not going to ever repay the money he owes me."

Now take your one sentence and repeat it ten times, each time putting this phrase in front of it: "I'm telling myself-(insert your assumption or belief)."

After repeating this 10 times...do you notice any change?

---

[10] This contemplation is adapted from work developed by The NVC (Nonviolent Communication) Training Institute.

YOUR BRAIN + CONFLICT
YOUR BRAIN IS:

- 3 pounds of tofu-like tissue.
- 1.1 trillion brain cells.
- 100 billion gray matter neurons.
- Always on: 24/7/365 .
- Reading instantly any information on demand.
- Speedy: Neurons firing around 5 - 50+ times per second.Signaling: neurons sending messages in a tenth of a second making 5000 connections with other neurons + 500 trillion synapses.

In other words, the brain is programmed to act fast and generates around 75,000+ thoughts a day.

THE TRIUNE BRAIN:
Three Critical Brain Actions

(1) AVOIDING (Reptilian Brain) Acts on autopilot to avoid being eaten or harmed and avoid danger. This was the earliest part of the brain that developed in humans. This part of the brain generates typical behaviors involved in aggression, dominance, territoriality and ritual displays (FIGHT, FLIGHT OR FREEZE).

(2) APPROACHING (Limbic Brain: Paleo-Mammalian) Allows us to approach resources for food, warmth and shelter, bonding and attachment, reproduction motivation and emotions involved in feeding, and parenting, reciprocity.

(3) ATTACHING (Neo Cortex Complex-Mammalian) Forms and maintains social networks; abstraction, imagination, thinking, planning & perception. The more sophisticated our social connections are, the larger our pre-frontal cortex is. This is the 'rational' part of the brain.

THE NEGATIVITY BIAS: VELCRO + TEFLON

- The negativity bias is the psychological and neurological reality by which humans pay more attention to, and give more weight to negative experiences rather than positive experiences or other kinds of information. Why? From the beginning of time we've needed to be able to sense danger to survive.
- Negative experiences produce more neural activity than equally intense (e.g., loud, bright) positive ones. They are also seen more easily and quickly.
- Negative experiences are immediately stored in long term memory, whereas positive experiences must be held in awareness for 12 or more seconds to to make it to our long term memory.
- Therefore our brains are set up to act like **VELCRO** for negative experiences (they stick in the minds for a long time) and like **TEFLON** for positive experiences (they slide right out of the mind).

Can you see how this might affect any conflicts you find yourself in? The bad news is, we remember the negative experiences, grudges and resentments we hold. We can get stuck in them. The good news is, we can practice balancing our brains with taking in the good (holding positive experience for at least 12 seconds in the mind), and working with practices like the one that follows. The other good news is, once we are aware that our brain operates on auto-pilot with negativity, we can practice mindfulness to catch these moments faster and work with increasing 'velcro-ing' the positive and 'teflon-ing' the negative.

"Why should I give them my mind as well?"
H. H. Dalai Lama, when asked why he wasn't angry at the Chinese
for taking over his country

MEDITATION:
SAFE, RESOURCED + CONNECTED

First, ground yourself with mindfulness of body and breath, sitting quietly, focusing on your body and the sensations of breathing – air moving across your nostrils, belly rising and falling, chest rising and falling, etc.

(Note: When learning this it may help to have your gaze down or eyes closed in an appropriate setting; however, this practice can be done with eyes wide open and gaze up.)

1)SAFE: Say silently to yourself:
"I am safe, I'm not in danger right now." Reflect on your current state of relative safety or freedom from danger and hold the feelings of safety in your mind for 30 seconds or more, repeating over and over for at least 30 seconds: "I am safe."

2) RESOURCED: Say silently: "I have what I need right now."
Reflect on your current state of having basically what you need in terms of food, warmth, shelter, etc. and hold the feelings of being resourced in your mind repeating over and over for at least 30 seconds: "I am resourced."

3) CONNECTED: Say to yourself: "I am connected to others."
Reflect on your current state of having personal relationships and hold the images and feelings of connectedness in your mind for 30 seconds or more repeating "I am connected."

TENSE + RELAX PRACTICE

Our bodies respond to conflict and stress with muscle tension, then our muscles become tense which creates more discomfort. "Tense & Relax" is a practice to use to relax the mind and body. Learning the clear difference between tension and relaxation in your body will help to be more alert when stressed, and signal you to relax.

THE PRACTICE:

- Lie down. Take a deep inhale. Suspend the breath.

- With the breath suspended, tense tightly every muscle in the body for a few seconds. Tense your fists, arms, legs, feet, scrunch your face, stomach, shoulders, toes and calves, as if you are squeezing every muscle in your body into your spine. HOLD for a few seconds, then relax with a large exhale.

- Do this three times.

- Then relax fully and scan your body. Notice any difference.

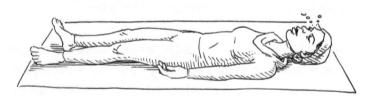

DEEP LISTENING PRACTICE

In conflict (and in all of life), listening is a deep practice. Creating space in your mind to listen—especially to those you think are enemies—can create a shift in the conflict dynamic. When someone gets it that we are are really listening to whatever is bothering them, things change for the better. Drop the thoughts and needing to quickly respond. Just listen.

PUSH + YIELD

Has physical or verbal fighting ever created trouble or messy conflicts for you? If so, one way to work with strong aggressive energy in ourselves and others is to learn how to notice the 'push and yield' energy that shows up in our bodies, minds and actions.

In the ancient eastern tradition of Taoism, and in particular the practice of Tai Chi, practitioners work with push and yield exercises. Tai Chi Instructor (and Path of Freedom facilitator) Mark Genco describes 'push and yield' practice:

"The basic point of the push and yield idea is that meeting force with force causes violence, conflict and destruction, like two cars smashing into each other. If one can learn to be like water and yield to whatever force, physical or non-physical, you can potentially win out of the situation with little or less pain, emotionally and physically."

Being able to hold your seat powerfully in response to aggressive or pushy energy is not weak, it is a great mark of strength. The most effective way to win in conflict is to yield. Yielding is not giving away power, it's about being calmly in our own power in any situation. We get this power by controlling our own responses and holding our seats.

In 'Push Hands,' a Taoist exercise. you learn how to yield (even while standing), because when you yield, the would-be aggressor has no where to put their aggression. It's as if the wild energy just passes right by you with no where to land. You've simply made a calm move back (or to the side) and simply watch it fall into space.

PUSH + YIELD EXERCISE

- Lie down, take a few deep breaths. Mentally scan your body and notice any tightness, and breathe into it to relax. Notice where your body feels open, relaxed or yielding.
- Roll over and experiment with pushing energy by using your arms to push the ground (push up). Notice how your body feels when pushing. Notice any difference.
- Stand up and imagine you are an actor playing out conflict. Enact a few of these conflict different styles, paying close attention to where your body begins to push or yield.
  - ARMORING: is not yielding, it's pushing back against yourself and others by creating blocking moves.
  - DEFENSE: striking or pushing back, how does this look and feel in the body?
  - COMPETITION: perhaps boxing (where you deliberately push and yield).
  - ESCALATING: full on fighting, pushing your energy into space.

Notice how you hold your body differently for each style. When does your energy feel pushy? What moves you to yield? Be precise with noticing the difference in your body.

During the next week notice when you or others are pushing their energy into space. Notice when you are more relaxing or yielding. Make a mental note of what kind of things trigger one or the other.

"Yea, every time I look at the Grand Canyon,
I'm reminded that the water won. Big Time!"
Gary Janko, Zen Priest

10. THE POWER OF FORGIVENESS

An "eye for an eye" has been a norm in the world even though this method has been proven to increase the amount of violence and hurt in our world. Forgiveness is a radical shift in view. It is through forgiveness that we as humans can truly begin to find the path of freedom.

WHAT IS FORGIVENESS?

Forgiveness is the choice to let go of resentment and bitterness. It's choosing to notice all that is good in your life that you can be grateful for. It's finding peace with the present moment instead of thinking endlessly about the past. Forgiveness is a process, not a single event, and so it can take time. It's your choice.

The Power of Forgiveness is the last chapter because it contains so much of what we explored in previous chapters. In the process of forgiving others we can come to terms with the fact that we can't control what others do. Forgiveness is not about letting people off the hook or denying reality, it's about letting go of feeling that it's our job to hold people accountable. With forgiveness you step out of the blame game and take ownership of any part you are responsible for in the situation.

Forgiveness is about choosing not to rent space in your head to people who don't care about you or may never even think about you. It's about moving into empowerment and out of a victim mindset. Forgiveness is for you and not others; so it's not always about reconciliation. It is entirely possible to forgive someone that we never see again. We forgive when we are ready, not when we (or others) think we 'should.'

Forgiveness is not the same thing as forgetting. We may never forget what happened, and when thoughts of past hurt come up, it is what we do with our minds, emotions and actions that matters.

OBSTACLES TO FORGIVENESS

- The Blame Game
- The Victim & Grievance Story
- Expectations & Unenforceable Rules

CHANGE THE CHANNEL MEDITATION

The thoughts jumping around in our minds can often seem like watching TV and endlessly flipping the channel. We have remote control of our minds though, and can choose what channel we stick with: the grievance channel, the soap opera channel, the horror movie channel, or the forgiveness, beauty, discovery, or learning channel. It's your choice. Fred Luskin, author of "Forgive for Good" says: "Focusing too much attention on a hurt makes it stronger and forms a habit that can be difficult to break. Dwelling on wounds gives them power over you."

TRY THIS SHORT MEDITATION:

- Think of a beautiful place in nature: beach, woods, mountains.
- Visualize this place: images, sounds, smells.
- Relax, and let your mind rest in this different 'channel.'

THE BLAME GAME

You can probably see how blaming others is not productive. The blame game gets us nowhere fast. If we think our problems are caused by someone or something else, then we have to look outside of ourselves for solutions. As we discussed in the Empowerment class, this approach gives all our power away. When we blame another person and get caught up in negative emotions, we are giving that person the power to control our emotions. It's much more empowering to shift the attention to what we can change, like our thoughts and reactions.

How much precious time in your life do you spend:

- Reflecting on your past rather than living in the present?
- Renting out space in your head to past wounds or to people who probably aren't even thinking about you?
- Wondering why people do what they do when you really have no way of knowing?
- Endlessly thinking about, elaborating, and even exaggerating the same old story?

VICTIM + GRIEVANCE STORIES

We all have bad memories and 'same old stories' that get repeated over and over and become grand stories of grievance. We've talked about the Victim position in the Drama Triangle chapter. But here the focus is how forgiveness can cut through our Victim and Grievance stories. What is happening when we get caught in a loop of grievances? Basically, we can't deal with the fact that we didn't get what we wanted (or we got what we didn't want!). As Fred Luskin says, we got a big "NO" when we wanted a "YES" from life. We might get caught in the injustice of it all for years, trying to make sense of it and trying to get everyone on our bandwagon of injustice. When we fall into the victim stance of grievance, we end up talking endlessly about our sad tale. We seek as many allies as we can who might agree with us (Rescuers). Some of us tell the same tired story for years or even decades. Never giving it up, we allow this tale of woe to become a part of our identity. It's not that bad things don't happen to people, of course they do. On the Path of Freedom, rather than getting caught in endless complaining, we work to let go of grievances once and for all.

One point to remember: every time you tell your grievance or victim story you are recreating the same stress reaction in your body that the original hurt created, which is why it feels so 'real' each time you retell it. Victim stories are not only a waste of precious time, but they are bad for your health and peace of mind. The bottom line is: do we really need to endlessly ruminate about someone who has probably moved on and doesn't even think about us anymore? Forgiveness is also about saying "NO!" and is a way to and move on to a better way of living.

"We habitually erect a barrier called blame that keeps us from communicating genuinely with others, and we fortify it with our concepts of who's right and who's wrong."
Pema Chodron, Author

EXPECTATIONS + UNENFORCEABLE RULES

Joan Halifax, spiritual teacher, says "Expectations are planned resentments." Dr. Fred Luskin calls expectations "unenforceable rules." When you have trouble forgiving, you are at the resentment stage. When we refuse to forgive someone we are caught up in our own ideas about how they should or shouldn't have behaved. Examining the expectations or unenforceable rules we set up in our heads will go a long way toward cutting any resentments we might have in the future. Take a moment and ask yourself, "What are some examples of expectations or rules I create that I expect others to obey?" Maybe it's that everyone should respect you. Perhaps it's that your partner should show up for you. Or that your friends or family should treat you better. Maybe you think that today is the day everything should be different. Basically, anytime we hear the word 'should' we are in the expectations and unenforceable rules realm.

The only person you really have control over is yourself. You can ask people to do things and they might do them, but basically they are going to do what they want to do. When we get the idea that we can control someone else's thinking and behavior with our own unenforceable rules, expecting them to do what we want, we are setting ourselves up for rolling out another possible victim story of resentment.

Not to say that all these things are not reasonable wishes, but when we demand that they happen and freak-out when they don't, we are fighting against our own expectations. We are basically trying to force change on things that we have no power to actually change, and frustrating ourselves in the process!

Anytime we are even mildly unhappy with someone or something, we are in the Victim position. The same thing applies with this concept: any time you are upset with someone else, you most likely have an expectation or unenforceable rule in play. Check out whether this makes sense. Challenge your expectations and unenforceable rules.

"An 'Unenforceable Rule' is an expectation you have for how something should turn out or how someone should think or behave. We have as much chance of enforcing our unenforceable rules as of getting blood out of a stone."
Fred Luskin, Forgive for Good

STEPS TO FORGIVENESS

- **LET IT GO:** It's in your own self-interest not to live in bitterness and anger. Realize that peace of mind is more important than resentment. Move on.

- **MINDFULNESS:** Get into the now – this alone can cut through a lot of the rumination and elaboration that goes with maintaining resentments. Be, here, now with what is happening, not with what you want to happen or what you think should have happened.

- **OWNERSHIP:** Own your part of the situation. Again, we aren't talking about beating yourself up, but simply acknowledging your part. Verbalize it if it seems appropriate and move on. Identify the Feelings and Unmet needs we talked about in the Communication Class.

- **FORGIVE YOURSELF:** Everyone makes mistakes.

- **CHALLENGE YOUR GRIEVANCE STORIES:** change your story from the Victim to the Hero. Forgiveness itself is a heroic act. Own it.

- **QUESTION AND CHALLENGE** your own ideas about what people 'should' do as we discussed in the "Who Am I?" class.

- **BECOME AWARE** when you are stuck in 'expectations' of others and let them go before they turn into resentments.

- Lastly, and most importantly: **CONNECT WITH ALL THE POSITIVE INTENTIONS IN YOUR LIFE:** What is it you really want? Connect with your own nobility and all of your positive dreams and goals.

FORGIVENESS MEDITATION

This is a great practice to do when you are in the heat of anger, regret, and blame and need to feel empathy and/or forgiveness for yourself and others. Take a comfortable seat. Focus your attention on the breath. Rather than cutting your thoughts, allow them to drift freely in and out of your mind. Remember a situation when you did something for which you think you cannot forgive yourself.

Repeat each line silently three times:

> "I forgive myself for whatever I did in the past."
> "I forgive myself for my actions."
> "I forgive myself for my words and my thoughts that caused pain or hurt."
> "If I cannot forgive myself now, may I be able to do so in the future."
> "May I be happy and find peace."

Now, visualize a person you want to forgive, someone you resent or feel negative about and say this to yourself:

> "I forgive you for what you did."
> "I forgive your actions, your words that caused me pain."
> "I forgive you and ask that you forgive me for whatever part I played."
> "If I cannot forgive you now, may I be able to in the future."
> "May you be happy and find peace."

Repeat three times. Even if it seems impossible for this to be true, do it, imagining that this message is received and accepted. Notice if you have a shift or reaction to this practice. Try not to get caught in judgment. This is an intense practice that may take time to land. Keep practicing and let the effects settle into your being. You won't regret it.

SELF-FORGIVENESS MEDITATION

Imagine a situation where you did something you think was bad, something you might even feel guilt, shame, or regret about.

Breathe in. Mentally say "I accept total responsibility for my actions and I request forgiveness."

(Try not to go into the story here - no blame, no justifications, no fear. Simply repeat the statement on the in-breath).

Breathe out. Mentally say "I send out forgiveness, healing, and understanding."

Do this at least 10 times.

Through this practice you are breathing in responsibility and breathing out forgiveness and understanding. Keep it simple. If memories and visualizations of the person or situation arise, simply return to the breath and resume the statements.

After finishing the repetitions, simply sit, watching the in and out-breath for at least 5 minutes.

"The moment in which the mind says: 'This isn't what I wanted, but it's what I got' is the point at which suffering disappears. Sadness might remain, but the mind is free."
Sylvia Boorstein, Author

MINDFULNESS IN ACTION
STAYING FREE THROUGH MINDFUL LIVING

II TIPS FOR MINDFUL LIVING

I. MINDFULNESS OF BODY:
Develop a habit of stopping several times a day to check-in for tension. Notice where you feel tense and take a deep breath.

> PAYOFF: Being present, reducing stress, increasing relaxation.

2. MINDFULNESS OF SPEECH:
When talking with others, if you find yourself checking out, stop and just listen. Listen to tone of voice, the words, the feelings, and the needs that are being communicated.

> PAYOFF: People appreciate it when others listen, relationships improve.

3. MINDFULNESS OF THOUGHTS:
Make a habit of checking in with yourself and noticing your thoughts. If your thoughts are not peaceful or are judgmental—

just notice them as if you are a witness. Take a few deep breaths. Notice any judgments and let them go. Notice any urge to act on thoughts and just watch.

> PAYOFF: A less judgmental mind and more self-awareness. Ability to choose your response with care.

4. MINDFULNESS OF EMOTION:
If you have a negative emotion, stop and label it - e.g. "frustration," "anger," "sadness," etc. No need to avoid emotions, just notice them. Emotions will pass like birds in the sky if you don't make a big deal out of them with a lot of extra thinking.

> PAYOFF: Less reactivity, more resilience, and the ability to see emotions as impermanent.

5. MINDFULNESS OF DAILY ACTIVITIES:
During your day, bring attention to anything you do on autopilot. Example: brushing your teeth, making the bed, washing hands, etc and bring awareness to all the sensations involved. Notice textures, temperatures, pressure, sounds, muscles contracting and releasing, the play of light and shadow, etc.

> PAYOFF: Routine activities make up a lot of life. Becoming present while doing the "boring" brings brings energy to our daily life.

6. MINDFUL MOVEMENT:
When you are working out or exercising, notice your breathing. Notice if it becomes labored, fast, shallow, or deep. Simply notice.

> PAYOFF: Tuning into how your body responds when you put extra demands on it allows you to become more aware of your limits and be more clear about when (or when not) to push those limits.

7. MINDFUL STANDING: As you are standing in line waiting, bring attention to your body, feel your feet, and take a deep breath.

> **PAYOFF**: Developing patience and the ability to simply be in the 'now,' free from frustration and expectation.

8. MINDFUL EATING:
Many of us eat unconsciously, barely noticing what we put in our mouths, and rarely tasting our food beyond the first bite. Try slowly tasting each bite. Appreciate how food fuels your body.

> **PAYOFF**: More relaxing meals, ability to enjoy the 'simple things' in life.

9. MINDFUL FREE TIME:
When you have time to 'do nothing' try simply meditating for a few minutes instead of daydreaming or seeking distraction.

> **PAYOFF**: Being fully present and enjoying your life more.

10 MINDFUL TV:
Do you ever mindlessly flip through TV on auto-pilot? Notice your emotions: does news create anxiety? Commercials make you cringe?

> **PAYOFF**: As you become more aware of how you "use" things like TV to numb ourselves, the more conscious we can be to choose watching for relaxation, rather than using it as a tool to escape life.

11. MINDFULNESS OF SPEED:
"Practice the 'philosophy of slow,'" suggests leadership expert Sally Helgesen. For example, walk a bit slower and be aware of your feet on the ground.

> **PAYOFF**: Slowing down reduces stress, builds patience and allows for clearer thinking.

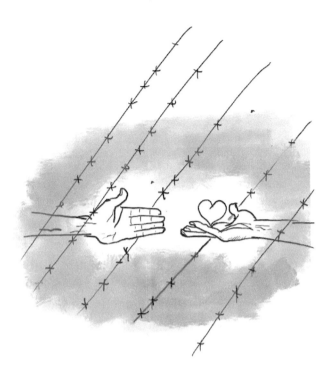

"We who lived in concentration camps can remember the men who walked through the huts comforting others, giving away their last piece of bread. They may have been few in number, but they offer sufficient proof that everything can be taken from a man but one thing: the last of the human freedoms—to choose one's attitude in any given set of circumstances, to choose one's own way."

Viktor Frankl, author, Man's Search for Meaning

THE PATH OF FREEDOM (POF) PROJECT

Kate (Vita Pires) Crisp created the Path of Freedom curriculum/ book/prison project in 2006. The curriculum was inspired by a training that Fleet Maull, Judith Gass and Kate developed in the early 2000's called the Integral Peacemaker Training (IPT). Kate, as the Executive Director of the Prison Mindfulness Institute (PMI), was inspired to develop a version of the IPT for prison classes. Thus the POF was born. PMI's team, in conjunction with Naropa University student/interns first piloted the POF in a juvenile facility and Kate taught it at a women's prison class in Colorado.

To date, there are POF prison classes in over 25 countries where thousands of prisoners have been trained in the content. Prison Mindfulness Institute has run an Intro to the Path of Freedom online course since 2009 that over 1000 people from around the world have completed.

Visit prisonmindfulness.org for more information.

ACKNOWLEDGEMENTS

Many thanks to all the dedicated and generous volunteers and staff who over the years have helped develop and adapt this program and curriculum for at-risk and underserved populations.

Special thanks to Dr. Fleet Maull, Dr. Amber Kelly, Rebecca Foster, Gary Schapiro, Susan Phenix, Nealy Zimmerman, Debra Callahan, Marge Houy, Micah Thanhauser, and Madrone Phoenix for their input and feedback on the curriculum.

Much thanks to Dr. Steven Karpman, Dave Emerald, Judith Ansara Gass, and Dr. Fred Luskin who graciously allowed their material to be adapted for this book.

Extra special thanks to: the pioneer group of Path of Freedom prisoner facilitators in Rhode Island and Washington State; to the POF participants at the ACI Cranston; the young men who attended the first POF Pilot program at Lookout Mountain Youth Facility; and the women at the Boulder County Jail and Rhode Island ACI, all who all provided great inspiration for further development of the POF.

Special thanks to illustrators Art Reid and Samo Skerbec for their expertise and endless patience in the creation of the illustrated version.

Extending deepest appreciation to the Kalliopeia Foundation, Mindful Connections Foundation, and The Trust for the Meditation Process for generously funding the Path of Freedom project.

Lastly and most importantly, I dedicate the merits and fruit of this project to all the thousands of people in prisons all around the world who have attended Path of Freedom classes.

Kate Vita Pires-Crisp, April 2020. Deerfield, MA